T0066942

VIETNAM AND BACK

Every Wake-up is a Good Day

PHIL HITCHCOCK

VIETNAM AND BACK
EVERY WAKE-UP IS A GOOD DAY

iUniverse books may be ordered through booksellers or by contacting:

iUniverse
1663 Liberty Drive
Bloomington, IN 47403
www.iuniverse.com
1-800-Authors (1-800-288-4677)

ISBN: 978-1-4917-3819-1 (sc)
ISBN: 978-1-4917-3820-7 (e)

Library of Congress Control Number: 2014910858

Printed in the United States of America.

iUniverse rev. date: 7/21/2014

For:

Bill C, Frank B, Joe W, Bob K, other friends and pilots in my flight school class who did not come back.

CONTENTS

PREFACE

This book was written to pass on to those who may be interested in the Vietnam War, the experiences and impressions from my year flying helicopter gunships in Vietnam during the late '60s. My Vietnam experience was an intense and exciting time. It was life changing. When writing letters home most detail regarding the deadly day to day combat action was intentionally avoided. Everyone was seeing daily updates on the war on TV and there was no point causing unnecessary worry. As a result, my family and friends knew very little about the combat action and the events in which I was routinely involved. Over the years there has been little talk about Vietnam other than a few quick stories related on occasion. Interestingly, there has never been much curiosity demonstrated or many questions asked.

Another reason for writing this book is to preserve this story in print, lasting well beyond a few short conversations. It can be read, reread, pondered over, and read at one's own leisure. It will also serve as a record of many events from an important time in our history from the eyes of one individual U.S. Army helicopter gunship pilot. All the events and actions detailed in this book are typical to most helicopter gunship pilots in Vietnam. Nothing here is particularly extraordinary. The intent of this book is not to portray larger than life events or to create a sensational story, but rather to relate the activities of one average guy involved in helicopter warfare. If the reader does not want to be exposed to some details of combat actions in Vietnam, he should stop reading now and put the book down.

United States involvement in Vietnam was very unpopular. And the negative mood regarding the Vietnam experience seems to be a lasting one. More recently however, the Vietnam conflict might be viewed as having been justifiable, when considering the significant collapse of communism worldwide. We should keep in mind that in the mid 1960's communism was a real threat. At the time though, our involvement in Vietnam appeared to be a total waste of money, and sadly, a waste of more than 58,000 American lives. It still may be thought by some to have been a total waste. We should also remember the hundreds of thousands of Vietnamese who died and the thousands upon thousands of Vietnamese still reported missing in action today.

This book has been written following the general chronology of my year in Vietnam, along with periods leading up to going over, and the period immediately after returning home. Names for the enemy used are: VC (Viet Cong}, NVA (North Vietnamese Army), Charlie (generally the VC or NVA) and bad guys.

Full names of people referenced in this book have been avoided to protect their identities and any possible sensitivity of their families.

No one knows very much about my experiences in Vietnam. So, although it has felt more comfortable remaining anonymous up to this point, it is now time to tell a more complete story.

Phil Hitchcock, Captain, U. S. Army, Vietnam 28 January 1969 to 28 January 1970.

ACKNOWLEDGMENTS

Margaret, my lovely wife, has been a major part of my life for the past many years and has been a most willing participant in everything we have chosen to do together, from working in our Aviation Contract Services business, to pursuing our aerial photography adventures, to building a sailboat and going sailing. We have spent many hours in totally open and honest conversation bearing our hearts and souls. I have let down my guard, torn down the brick wall, and she now knows me better than any other person. She has spent countless hours editing this writing and has suggested many important changes. She is truly my life's partner.

I want to thank Joel Henderson, AECS U.S. Navy, retired. Joel is a long time friend from my flying days and has contributed information about the Navy in Vietnam and other specifics of Navy ship designations and missions. Joel served two tours in Vietnam and spent some time in Dong Tam and surrounding areas where I also served.

Thanks to my sister, Jane, for reading my manuscript and offering several suggestions for improvement. Her comments regarding overall content and readability have been helpful.

PROLOGUE

It was another sunny day late in the afternoon, in South Vietnam. I had just positioned my gunship at an altitude of 3,000 feet above my target and was in a steep dive launching rockets as fast as the trigger could be pulled. The target was a long canal with palm trees on both sides where Viet Cong lived and were hiding in tunnels. This was the location where Frank, another captain and a friend of mine, had been killed a few days before by enemy fire. We were delivering some extra punishment on the bad guys. I fired twenty rockets before reaching maximum airspeed and began pulling out of my dive. Turning hard left into a steep climbing turn back up to altitude, I set up for another attack. Reaching altitude we performed a wing-over maneuver and rolled back on target in another steep dive. Eighteen more rockets were launched in the few seconds it took to reach maximum airspeed. After making another hard left turn and starting the climb back to altitude heading back to base, there was suddenly a loud explosion. The gunship shuddered and the cockpit immediately filled with white smoke. We were hit hard, and I felt the blast from under my seat on the back of my legs. The VC were known to have shoulder fired B40 rockets in this area, and we were always alert, watching out for the threat.

I immediately reduced power and headed toward the ground, our ultimate refuge. Moving the flight controls around back and forth revealed that they were still functioning okay. When the smoke cleared, a quick scan of the instrument panel indicated that all systems appeared to be operating normally. While applying power and stopping our descent, the gunship seemed to be flying okay. Once again we began our climb to altitude heading back toward base. At first glance, there appeared to be no injury to my legs. Looking around the helicopter quickly, I noticed a hole about the size of a softball through the lower part of my door, about a foot away from my seat. There were ragged, torn metal edges outlining the hole. We continued on back to base and landed safely. This was one more close call, one of many past, and one of many more to come.

My time in Vietnam, actually had its beginning many years before.

CHAPTER 1

THE BEGINNING

Looking back to a time well before going into the military will reveal to some extent how future events developed and played out. My interest in flying began back in high school. I picked up a U.S. Army aviation promotional flyer somewhere and kept it with me, reading it and pondering the possibilities for several years. Subscribing to *Flying* magazine and reading it cover to cover every month fueled the fire. A noted psychologist has said that whatever you think about all the time, over a long period, will surely come to pass. Without fully realizing what was evolving, a path pursuing a growing thirst for adventure was developing, with the result being flying helicopter gunships in Vietnam.

Attending Western Michigan University's Aviation Engineering program, Army ROTC, and the ROTC Flight Program paved the way. I earned my Private Pilot's License in 1965 and received a commission as a 2nd Lieutenant into the Army in June 1967.

The military draft was a big deal for all young men in the mid-sixties due to the buildup of troop levels in Vietnam. Many guys were taken out of college, given a few weeks of training, handed a rifle, and sent to Vietnam. Not a good deal at all in my opinion. This was a risk all guys like me faced at this time. Others were drafted right after graduation from college. Some friends of mine were drafted and with few options were sent to Vietnam. I wanted to have more control of my immediate future and considered long and hard the choices before me.

One choice was to go through ROTC at Western. R.O.T.C. stood for Reserve Officer Training Corps. ROTC existed only at colleges and universities. The sole purpose was training of military officers over a four year period before being assigned to an active duty tour. The Army, Navy and Air Force each had ROTC programs at various schools around the country. I signed up for the first two years of basic ROTC during my freshman and sophomore years at Western that everyone could take with no further military obligation. A decision to enter advanced ROTC during my junior and senior years would mandate at least two years of active duty in the military as a Commissioned Officer after graduation. Importantly, it also offered a draft exemption during the additional years required to complete college. I was giving it serious consideration. One of my favorite instructors in ROTC, Captain Miller, took me aside one day and told me that he would personally break my arm if I didn't go on and get my commission into the Army. It was an interesting conversation. It was very meaningful to me and Captain Miller was really supportive. His comments settled the indecision in my mind. He saw my potential. After much thought and discussion with other Army instructors at Western, I decided to continue on and enter the two additional years of advanced ROTC. Once in advanced ROTC, and exempt from the draft, I could stay in college without interruption and get my degree. That solved one important issue.

I also wanted to fly, and the ROTC Flight Program was a direct route to flying in the military. So, my two objectives would be met, to graduate with a degree, and become a military pilot. Going to Vietnam was almost a certainty. It would be a whole lot better flying than trying to survive in the jungle on foot. As much as I liked the outdoors, walking around in the jungle would not be a fun place to be.

Signing my life away, literally, to be able to go to military flight school, I was on the way to becoming a military pilot. An extra year on active duty would also be required beyond the normal two years. After active duty, I would be subject to recall back into the military at any time during my lifetime. I knew what I was doing, I thought, and knew where I was likely headed. For a quiet, naïve country boy from Hickory Corners, Michigan, it was becoming a grand adventure.

I considered transferring to the Air Force or Navy after getting my commission, and flying with one of them. An inter-service transfer is something that was possible, and it was checked out. I probably would have ended up flying cargo or some other larger aircraft other than fighter jets however because of my above average height. That would have been okay but at the time new prospective pilots had an eye toward the hotter more exciting stuff. Fighters were, and still are, built for average sized guys with limited sitting height so they can wear their helmet and other gear and have the necessary clearance in the cockpit. Nearly all fighter jocks are six feet tall or less and of average build. Not being real interested in flying buses, I decided to stay in the Army and fly with them.

I did apply for fixed wing flight school where flying the Caribou STOL cargo plane, or the Mohawk, the high performance turbo prop reconnaissance plane, was possible. Not getting my fixed wing request though, as I suspected might be the case, I was eventually heading off to primary helicopter flight school at Ft. Wolters, Texas. Helicopters would be a great challenge and a new experience, so it was okay.

CHAPTER 2

GOING ON ACTIVE DUTY

Entering active duty at Ft. Knox, Kentucky in early December, 1967, for four months of Armor Officer Basic, was the boots-on-the-ground beginning of my military experience. Every commissioned officer in the Army has a basic branch assignment even though he may become a pilot. If he washed out of flight school for some reason, he would then go back to his basic area of training and command combat operations as a ground commander. I had applied for armor school while still in ROTC, which involved commanding combat tanks, commonly referred to as tin cans and sixty ton coffins. Involved with and training in those heavy machines was interesting but uneventful. Being a tank unit commander was not the sort of future I had in mind.

After completion of my Armor Officer Basic I was assigned to temporary duty at the airport at Ft. Knox to wait for my flight school starting date. The LOH Test Project was my temporary assignment which lasted for a few months. The LOH, light observation helicopter, was a new small jet turbine powered helicopter made by Hughes Aircraft with the military designation of OH6. Most people recognize it by its egg shape. It was small, fast and I had a chance to fly it some with other pilots. It was a real kick in the pants. It would accelerate from a stationary hover just above the ground to 100 miles an hour airspeed in about five seconds. The mission of the test project was to fly the four OH6's assigned to the unit a prescribed number of hours a week to determine part longevity and to establish standard time change schedules for various parts of the helicopter. The unit had a crew of pilots who flew the helicopters a lot. Flying with these pilots was great experience for me prior to starting helicopter flight training. We flew all over central Kentucky low level, often right on the tree tops, down gorges, over rivers, up hills and off cliffs. It was exciting. I was really impressed with this small helicopter.

As an officer I was able to take my wife with me into the military to Ft. Knox. We lived off base in a rented trailer. Enlisted guys or draftees were not allowed to have their wives with them when they initially went in the military. Because my pay was low while on temporary duty waiting for flight school, we were strapped for cash, and my wife was pregnant and not working. But we survived. There would be more lessons in survival in the months and years ahead.

CHAPTER 3

FLIGHT SCHOOL

With orders finally in hand to flight school, we departed Ft Knox in March,1968, and headed down to U.S. Army Primary Flight School at Ft. Wolters, in Mineral Wells, Texas. We drove our blue Mustang convertible, pulling a trailer behind with all our worldly possessions. We didn't need much and didn't have much.

We lived off base again in a rental trailer just outside of Weatherford, Texas, on a knoll overlooking the wide open Texas countryside. A nice place I thought, and it got hot at times. Good training. Copperhead snakes were common in the dry creek bed behind our house. We used to go for walks back there with tall boots. The name Copperhead would hold special significance for me later on as it turned out.

I began receiving flight pay which was an extra thousand dollars a month on top of my base pay of about six hundred a month. We had full medical, PX and commissary privileges on base, so our costs were fairly low. All of a sudden we were flush, financially.

The Army Primary Helicopter Flight School training helicopter that I flew was the Hiller OH23. It was an old model of helicopter from back in the Korean War days. It had the classic bubble canopy on the front, was powered by a piston aircraft engine, and would carry three people sitting side by side on one bench type seat. It looked similar to the helicopter we've all seen on the old MASH television series. It was quite strong, structurally speaking, and new helicopter students routinely beat them up with some poor flying techniques. Ft. Wolters had about 400 of these helicopters on one airfield.

The process of flying on and off the airfield with hundreds of other students at various times throughout the day was fascinating and was a little dangerous. A few flight school students died while I was at Ft. Wolters, in midair collisions or when they hit something and crashed. I had an engine failure once due to fuel that was contaminated with water. In later years I would fly an earlier model of this same OH23 with the Tennessee National Guard that had wooden rotor blades, believe it or not. It was basically a museum piece.

In May our first child was born at the base hospital at Fort Wolters. I was flying out in the boonies that day and someone had to track me down to inform me I was about to become a father. I was able to return to base in time for the delivery of a beautiful baby girl.

It was a hot summer out on the Texas prairie but it was a good time. I was gone pretty much from sunup to sundown in flight school during the week, with weekends off. We traveled around Texas some and saw the countryside. It was a nice place, and I came to like Texas with the open spaces, big blue sky and warm weather. It felt like a second home somehow. It still does.

At the completion of flight school at Ft. Wolters in August, 1968, I graduated top of my flight school class as honor graduate, establishing some of the highest inflight performance ratings and academic scores on record. It helped that I had an aviation engineering degree. A natural ability for flying also had been discovered, particularly flying the helicopter. It was challenging and fun.

I transferred from primary flight school in Texas to advanced flight school at Ft. Rucker, Alabama, spending another four months learning to fly the much larger Huey helicopter. The Huey helicopter, manufactured by Bell Helicopter, Ft. Worth, Texas, came in several models from the A model made in earlier years to the more current D model. We mainly flew the later D model at Ft. Rucker. The D model was powered by a 1,100 shaft horse power jet turbine engine. The helicopter had one large 40 foot diameter main rotor and a tail rotor. The body of the helicopter was fairly large and would carry ten or twelve people including a standard crew of four. Most people are very familiar with the look of this helicopter. It was the principle troop carrying helicopter used in Vietnam.

We initially started flying the Huey with a flight instructor learning all the basics of flight control and emergency procedures. After several hours and with the necessary demonstrated proficiency, we were organized into teams of two student pilots who then flew together practicing everything we had learned. There was no flight instructor on board at this point, just two student pilots. It was the "stick buddy" system. Being more proficient than some, I initially was assigned a stick buddy who was an Iranian Air Force student. His name was Javadi. He had a difficult time speaking English and had some problems with flight training both in the classroom and in the air. He was a great guy and we talked a lot. I very much functioned as an instructor pilot with Javadi, routinely keeping him out of all sorts of potential trouble. Later I flew with Bob K. as my stick buddy. We lost him in Vietnam.

Tactical instrument flight training was also provided at Ft. Rucker, and again I finished at the top of my class. Toward the end of flight school an additional gunship pilot training course was offered which was accepted with delight. The types of missions flown and the action involved was similar to flying fighter jets in some ways, but in helicopters. Not as fast, obviously.

Late in our advanced flight school training, all pilots were scheduled to visit the JAG office on base. The Judge Advocate General's office was in charge of completing all the paperwork that was necessary before our going to a combat zone. We completed such things as a Last Will and Testament, life insurance forms, recorded next of kin information and such. It was a bit sobering. The *doing* phase was getting closer.

We also got a lot of shots during this time, in an effort to prevent getting all sorts of strange diseases to which we would be exposed. I got seven shots in one session, four in one arm and three in the other. Nothing would make us bulletproof though. We asked for a shot for that but were told it hadn't been developed yet.

Before graduating from flight school in December, 1968, other paperwork was completed and I officially volunteered for Vietnam duty in writing. It didn't amount to much actually since I knew where I was going anyway, but it would look good on my record if a long term military career was chosen. Additional schooling in aircraft maintenance management was available to become an aircraft maintenance officer, but I decided to go on over to Vietnam and get my tour over with. The prospect of flying in combat was an exciting lure. Looking back, I should have taken advantage of the additional schooling. It would have significantly expanded a career path that had already started with my college degree. One should never pass up more educational opportunities. Hind sight is always pretty good. It can be important to give more than just casual thought to some decisions.

So flying gunships in Vietnam was soon to become reality. It would turn out being much like flying fighter jets in fact, firing a variety of attack weapons, but much more up close and personal, something some Air Force fighter jocks would later express they envied. It was time to go use my training and be tested well beyond the classroom.

I was scheduled for a one month leave before heading over to the sunny vacation land across the pond, so we packed up and traveled back to Michigan. My young family would be staying in our nice new mobile home in Kalamazoo, near family, while I was overseas.

My month off in January, 1969, was a bit stressful for both my wife and me, although we didn't talk about it much. It was understandable. We put things in order for my year away. We were living in our new mobile home just outside Schoolcraft, south of Kalamazoo. It was a pretty nice place. We spent a lot of time together with our baby girl and with family. Nearly all our time was spent together, which was unusual after spending so much time apart when I was in the rigorous flight school routine.

As it got closer to actual departure time, things got even tenser. It was difficult knowing how to react in those last few days. At one point my wife ran out of patience and blurted out, "I just wish you'd go." Although a little surprised, I understood. We both had a similar feeling. It was time to get on with it.

CHAPTER 4

GOING OVER

My folks took my wife, young daughter and me to the airport in Lansing, Michigan for my departure, in late January of 1969. We waited around in the terminal building for the call to board the commuter plane to Chicago. I don't remember that any of us had much to say. It was coming down to the wire. I was heading out into a big unknown, into a war zone. It was apparent that we all had mixed feelings, not quite knowing what to say or what to do. None of us had been through this before as we stood outside on the ramp to say our good-byes. Being late January, it was cold, and it was dark. We all had a few tears in our eyes as we kissed, hugged and said good-bye. It had come time to simply turn around and walk away. We knew it could be our last good-bye.

I was traveling with Joe W., a guy from Lansing who had been in my flight school class. We had become closely acquainted over the previous six or eight months. He was saying his good-byes to his wife of a couple of years. It would be the last time they ever saw each other, but they didn't know it at the time. War can really suck sometimes.

Joe and I walked to the plane, up the steps, and found seats on board. We looked out the window as the plane taxied away for takeoff. Although we'd had a lot of training, we really had no idea what we had gotten ourselves into. It was exciting in a strange sort of way. We planned to spend four days in San Francisco to see the sights and eat a lot of the last American food we would have for a long time. I remember feeling very alone somehow but strangely free and independent.

Thinking back, my wife may have felt abandoned, but she was certainly prepared for and understood what was happening. She was a fairly tough woman. It was no doubt becoming a grand adventure for her too, whether she liked it or not.

Joe and I got better acquainted during our time in San Francisco. We stayed in a hotel on Fisherman's Wharf. He was a good guy. He mentioned one time that he had been to a religious seminary school for a short time but became disillusioned with it, then transferred to a university and got a degree.

We ate out for every meal, visited the sights around San Francisco, rode the trolley cars, bummed around the wharf, and visited some salty dog sailor pubs. We ran out of money after a few days and had to go to the Presidio, the Army base in San Francisco, and request a pay advance. I was surprised they actually gave us cash. I then ran out of money again, and had to borrow another twenty five dollars from Joe.

We planned to spend all our money stateside because we couldn't have or spend American dollars in Vietnam. It was valuable international currency that was kept out of enemy hands. Vietnamese currency, the piaster and dong, were not worth much. We would be issued MPC, Military Pay Certificates. It was not backed by gold I can assure you. MPC was all paper money, even small change like 5 cents, 10 cents, and 25 cents. The paper certificates were all small in size, much like Monopoly money. How appropriate! We could have a big wad of paper in our pocket and only have a few bucks. It was accepted all over, even off base in local towns and villages. It could be exchanged for the Vietnamese dong and piaster.

We flew out of Travis Air Force Base on a TWA military charter on the 28th of January, 1969. The flight left very late at night. Most of the members of our flight school class went over together on the same flight, along with some other guys. Some of the guys arrived at Travis heavily under the influence and packed extra bottles of booze in their bag for the flight. The plane was packed with military guys in uniform. How the plane, a Boeing 707, managed to get off the ground had to involve a small miracle. They must have a very long runway there at Travis. It was dark, so we couldn't see much out the windows as we rolled down the runway and took off. We just blasted off into the black unknown. How fitting. The whole assembly and departure process was quite surreal. It is a blur now and the details almost nonexistent in my memory. It was only the beginning. The slate was blank and would be heavily written on in the year to come.

It was a long flight halfway around the world. Actual flight time was about nineteen hours. We crossed several time zones traveling through a sort of disorienting time warp. We only stopped twice for fuel, believe it or not. We stopped in Guam and Japan. That 707 could go forever on a load of fuel.

Guam was an interesting stop. It's basically a US Air Force island with a large base in the middle that B52s flew out of on bombing runs into Vietnam. There was a dark, low, cloud layer overhead and it was raining. We saw many black, spooky looking B52s on the ramp that were obviously working airplanes. The runway went almost from one side of the island to the other and must have been five miles long. It appeared as wide as many small airport runways were long here in the States. It was quite a sight.

The stop in Japan was at a commercial airport somewhere. Maybe Tokyo. We stopped in Tokyo on the way back a year later as well, where a nice watch was purchased for my wife, before continuing home. We got a new flight crew in Japan on the current

TWA charter that would take us on into Ton Son Khut airport in Saigon. The stewardesses were quite entertaining on our last leg to the war zone. One of them walked up and down the aisle with a centerfold picture from *Playboy* magazine pinned to her back. It was obviously her. You could tell from her smile!

After many hours and a very long flight, we finally landed in Saigon. We came to a stop on the runway, and everyone was scrambling to gather up what few personal items they had scattered around the plane, getting ready to disembark. The plane smelled like a locker room. The whole place had a very different look as we watched out through the windows and taxied to a parking place on the ramp. It appeared very slummy. We were all excited and wanted to get out of that confining airplane and back on the ground.

The door opened and we worked our way forward to the stairs that led down. I finally stepped out the door, and *WHAM*. The heat hit me in the face like opening the door to a blast furnace. It made an initial impression that has lasted over the years. It was hot, and it stunk. It smelled like a garbage dump.

We walked across the ramp and got on special military busses with grenade screens covering the windows. There was no air conditioning. The busses traveled through smelly, congested streets full of very different looking people going about their very different lives, to the 90th Replacement Battalion. It was fascinating.

The 90th Replacement Battalion was a small military compound at Ben Hoa, a nearby suburb of Saigon, where army pilots were processed in and out of country. As we stepped off the bus there was a large group of Vietnamese kids crowded around the door begging for money. A gang of poor kids begging was a very different, first time experience for me.

We signed in, and stayed at the replacement battalion for two days while the powers that existed decided where to send us individually now that we had actually shown up in person. Our bags were transferred from the airport on a military truck. We bunked down in a concrete block building in one large room that had open screens around the upper part of the walls. There was no air conditioning, and the local sounds and smells of the area flowed through day and night. We were confined to the compound.

There were mandatory briefings and orientations to attend while we waited for unit assignments. I elected to have most of my pay sent home to my wife on what was called an allotment. She was sent a check for around two thousand dollars each month and I was paid about two hundred a month in cash. Combat hazardous duty pay was now received in addition to my basic monthly pay and monthly flight pay. Not much money would be needed in Vietnam, just a few bucks for sundry items from the PX like toothpaste, maybe a bad bottle of wine, hair cuts, and dinner at the officer's club once in a while. Everything was cheap.

One of the forms we filled out was a Notification Election Form. On this form we chose how our next of kin were to be notified in case something happened to us. There were a few options. I elected to have my wife and folks notified on the same basis. If injured or wounded in some minor way, they were not to be notified. If injured or wounded more seriously, but not life threatening, they were not to be notified. In this case, they could be informed by letter with an explanation of what had happened. If injured or wounded with injuries that were life threatening, then they were to be notified. If killed in action, then of course they would be notified.

The guys I had just spent the last several months training with would all be sent to different places in Vietnam. Few of us would be stationed together. I would never see many of those guys from my flight school class again after departing the replacement battalion. Welcome to Vietnam.

CHAPTER 5

DONG TAM, A FASCINATING NEW PLACE

On a sunny morning, three days after leaving the good ole' U.S. of A, all of the guys that flew over with me stood in line in front of an officer sitting at a folding green table in the courtyard between the block buildings. We were getting our individual unit assignments to locations all over Vietnam. Our flight class was finally being broken up, with each of us becoming individual helicopter pilots heading off to war at some new and strange, but exciting place.

When my turn came at the green table, the officer went down his long list and actually found my name. *Amazing!* Dong Tam, and the 162nd Assault Helicopter Company was my assigned unit. "The hellhole of the south," he said, "in the Mekong Delta." *Thanks a lot.* All locations had their own unofficial descriptive names based to a significant degree on the facts. I had wanted to go up north and fly up in the mountains without actually knowing much about the area, except that it sounded beautiful. None of us were offered any choice. I was going to the southernmost Fourth Corps area, about 150 miles south of Saigon, and going there alone. No one else from my flight class was going to the same location.

Going south, as it turned out, to the mile upon mile of open flat rice paddies, would be a much safer place to fly than flying up north in the mountains. There were lots of areas for forced landings if you went down for some reason, and there would be many reasons in the upcoming months. Because it was farther away from North Vietnam, there also tended to be less intense enemy action. There was a greater distance for the enemy to move troops and weapons, and fewer areas of jungle for them to operate from.

I was told to be at a certain helipad at a certain time later that day to catch a courier flight to the 162nd Assault Helicopter Company, 13th Aviation Battalion, 1st Aviation Brigade, a unit totally unknown to me. I was told to check in at the company operations office upon arrival and sign in. The courier flight was a single helicopter, flying alone, that took over an hour almost directly south of Saigon to the Army base at Dong Tam. I was the only passenger on the flight. Dong Tam was near a small, ancient Vietnamese village named My Tho. This was my first helicopter flight in Vietnam. The sights were fantastic.

Dong Tam was located on the Mekong River a couple miles west of My Tho. The Mekong River was a main river out of Cambodia that split into two large tributaries, one heading east and one going southeast, both on the way to the South China Sea. This was the river made famous at one time because of all the dead bodies floating down it. That was after my time though.

After being dropped off at Dong Tam airfield, the courier flight departed, leaving me standing alone next to the runway with my one bag. Looking around at what would be my new home, I was in shock. The place looked really rough. A real hellhole. Everything was grayish brown and dirty looking: the ground, the buildings, the helicopter parking areas, the runway, everything. No buildings were painted. The only items painted were trucks, helicopters and other pieces of equipment in olive drab.

I walked the hundred yards or so around parked helicopters to Operations, checked in, and got about a fifteen minute briefing on the unit and our general mission. I was then assigned a room in the BOQ (bachelor officers' quarters) with a roommate, Dick G. He was the unit communications officer and a W2 Warrant Officer on his second tour to Vietnam. After dropping my bag in my hooch, and getting settled in a bit, I walked around to take a look at my new home and meet some of the guys. I didn't get any kind of tour from anyone. Our unit was located on the north side of the base where all the helicopters were parked in protective revetments along a 3,000 foot long PSP (perforated steel plate) runway. Refueling and rearming were located on the north side of the runway and we lived on the south side of the runway and the helicopter revetments.

After a long afternoon of exciting changes and an interesting first helicopter flight down from Saigon, I needed to pee. After looking around exploring the area, there was no obvious place to go. There were no restrooms or showers attached to, or in, our BOQ. There were a couple of rough looking buildings out in the middle of our open courtyard generally inside the L-shaped BOQ. I finally had to ask a guy where to take a pee. He said, "See that tube sticking up out there?" It was a rusty four inch diameter stove pipe sticking straight up out of the ground, about pecker high to a short guy, in the middle of the open dirt courtyard. It was totally out in the open. It was called a piss tube, a new term that hadn't been mentioned in any prior training. *Ah, beginning to learn new useful things already!* Being a country boy, I had no problem taking a leak outdoors, but this was a bit unique. A soldier would just saunter up on his way going somewhere, whip it out, and take a pee. No fuss, no muss. Very efficient. We had Vietnamese women and girls working in our unit in various jobs during the day who often walked by as we were standing at the tube. They did a good job pretending not to notice. It really didn't bother me after that first time.

One of the rustic looking buildings nearby was the "shitter" and it smelled "rustic", if rustic has a smell. I don't suppose you were supposed to do both in there. Anyway, the women and girls used the same shitter that we did while they were on base working during the day. They would yell out *choi oi* if you walked in on them. There were no latches on the door. I didn't understand much Vietnamese, but it was clearly an exclamation and protest of some sort. I soon learned to just walk on in to do my business while they scrambled to pull up their pants and take off. They didn't trust GI's much, at least not enough to share a shitter. Vietnamese could be downright antisocial sometimes!

The shitter set-up was an efficient way to dispose of human waste as it turned out, although it was a bit gross I suppose. It had a long box bench inside all along one wall with several toilet seats mounted above holes that went down below. Under each hole there was half of a fifty five gallon steel drum that had been cut in half with a cutting torch. When the drums got to be about two thirds full, something needed to be done, and you could tell. Since we lived in an area where the water table was only a couple of feet below the surface, the waste could not be dumped into the ground anywhere.

Vietnamese women come about once a week to process the waste. They would pull the cans out through doors in the back of the shitter, drag them about twenty feet away, and put "fresh" cans back in. They would then commence to do their job. They would take a few gallons of jet fuel, pour some into each can and stir it with wooden paddles making a flammable mixture. They lit the brew with matches and stood back. The black smoke billowed up and wafted through our whole company area, including our BOQ which was nearby. The black, oily smoke really stunk, and it looked really bad. We avoided it however we could. You haven't smelled stink until you've smelled burning human waste. It burned for an hour or so. We had few mosquitoes though! The women were fully dressed from head to toe with long sleeves, gloves of course, rags tied across their faces, and hats pulled down over their ears. I wonder why. Perhaps it was to protect their dignity. When the cans had burned out and were empty, the women stacked them for next time. This might not have been a high seniority job, if seniority existed, but perhaps it paid better than other work. It should have.

We had a 155 millimeter artillery battery located right next to our BOQ, maybe 100 yards away. The 155 mm Howitzer was the biggest artillery piece the Army had in Vietnam at the time and may still be the biggest. The 155 mm round is an explosive projectile about eight inches in diameter and about two feet long, and very heavy. Wouldn't you know it, they conducted their fire missions at night when normal people were trying to sleep. It was tough getting any sleep for a while. When they were actively firing, the blast every minute or so would literally rattle every board in our BOQ. I lived on the first floor. For a while, dirt rained down on us from the second floor through cracks in the floorboards every time they fired. I finally tacked up mosquito netting on our ceiling which helped cure the problem, catching most of the coarser dirt. After a while one learned to sleep through it.

My first month in Vietnam was quite a lonely experience and it took some time to get adjusted. I went alone to a completely foreign place, on the other side of the world, to a new organization where I didn't know anyone. Plucked suddenly out of one environment and one life and dropped into a totally new environment and a strange new life was quite an adjustment that took a few days. I toughened up mentally in a hurry. The people were friendly enough.

Having no prior information for my new address for mail until arriving at my new unit in Vietnam, there was no mail coming from home of course. I sent letters right away to my folks and my wife with my mailing address. Writing and mailing letters felt good. The mail took about two weeks each way, so my letters took two weeks to get home, then two more weeks before I would get return mail. It would be a full month, therefore, before getting any word from my previous life. Six or eight letters were sent home before I received my first letter. I looked forward to those first letters with some anticipation. Getting letters from home was a big deal for everyone in Vietnam. Written letters were the only form of communication. There was no satellite communication or email like today.

Making the decision right away to not include certain details of combat action in my letters home would protect everyone from unnecessarily worry. My letters would be whitewashed, in a sense, and only include nice things like the warm weather, the interesting people, the beautiful country, information about our unit, and the fun flying. I avoided reporting information about getting shot up, killing people, our people being injured or killed, and numerous near-miss incidents. I recognized this would leave everyone uninformed to a significant degree regarding what was happening, and what was being experienced, but I thought it would be for the best.

After a day or two getting acquainted with my new unit, several items of standard issue were given to me by our supply department in preparation to go to work. Included was a flight helmet, flight gloves, three sets of Nomex fire retardant flight suits, a Smith & Wesson .38 revolver to be carried as a personal weapon, ammunition, a "chicken plate", which was an armored vest worn in flight, and some other things. A supposedly bullet resistant ballistics flight helmet was available. It was made of extra thick laminated material that was supposed to stop a .30 caliber round if you were hit in the head. A nice thought. Most guys didn't use them because they were usually not available, and they were heavy. The extra protection sounded like a reasonable idea to me. A headache was a routine experience when flying for the next month due to the weight of the helmet, until the cushion pads inside were arranged so it was more comfortable.

With the helmet, the armored vest, the armored helicopter seat, and an armored flat panel that slid forward on the outside of side of the seat, there would be at least some protection from enemy gunfire. Enough guys were still hit by enemy bullets but the armor plating around us saved a lot of lives. Some guys were hit directly in the chest by enemy fire, and thanks to their armored vest, lived to tell about it.

A few days later, after meeting more people in our unit and getting better acquainted, I went out to fly with our unit flight instructor pilot. We flew a regular D model Huey around the area for about an hour so he could confirm that I was real and knew what was required to handle the helicopter properly and at fly safely. We ran though all normal flight operations and emergency procedures. My flying was good considering that I had not flown for almost two months. It felt great to be flying again.

Several days later I went out with another pilot on an area orientation flight. We flew in a little 4 seat LOH, light observation helicopter. It was designated an OH6, the same one our unit had flown when we were assigned temporarily to the LOH Test Project back at Ft. Knox waiting for my flight school date. It was the Hughes 300, a little egg-shaped turbine powered helicopter that was light, quick and fast. It would accelerate from a hover to about one hundred knots of airspeed in about five seconds. A real kick.

We flew most of the day around the area including up the border along Cambodia, two hundred miles or so off to the west. It was a beautiful sunny day and it was a great flight with an experienced pilot pointing out all the landmarks, villages, Special Forces bases, and such, that would be used later as reference when flying in our areas of operation. It was a beautiful helicopter tour. I carried a Smith & Wesson .38 caliber revolver, loaded for action that was issued to me for my personal protection. The weapon would make some noise but be almost a waste of time if one actually needed to protect himself. But it looked good hanging in my holster around my waist. *A real cowboy in the Wild West!*

A few weeks later this routine orientation flight was terminated because one flight never returned and was never found. It was a stark introduction to the fact that this was not a particularly safe flying environment. They could have been shot down, had an engine failure and crashed, or been captured and marched to North Vietnam to some prison. It was not a good, last orientation flight for those involved. I made it back from my flight okay, so life goes on.

The feeling of *Oh well, I'm still here, go back to work,* would become the attitude when fellow pilots or other members of our unit were injured or worse and not return from the day's missions. Something that happened all too often. Known risks were part of the work we were engaged in and we accepted the risks as a normal part of daily life. We felt bad of course when we lost people, but the next day somehow came around on schedule when we opened our eyes and saw the light of another day. Every wake-up was the beginning of a good day, comparatively speaking.

The Vietnamese men and women who worked on base had to leave base around five o'clock in the afternoon. *No Vietnamese on base at night*, was the rule. They were needed off base at night anyway, by the VC, to shoot mortars at us! It was great work for them on base and American pay was good. A part of winning hearts and minds you know.

We had hooch maids come in everyday to clean our hooches, do our laundry and polish our boots. A *hooch* was a general name for any place where a person lived, had all his stuff, cooked, slept, and read the *Wall Street Journal.* Ha! It could be a room in a large building, a building with a cot in it, a grass hut, whatever. The Vietnamese lived in hooches also. Our hooch maids didn't speak much, or any, English so it was fun trying to communicate with them. We ended up speaking a few Vietnamese words that we learned, and they learned a few English words, so we somehow understood each other in some basic conversations. It always took extra time and effort, and a lot of hand gestures. It was fun and we all had lots of laughs.

There were some wild stories about hooch maids and American guys as you could imagine, but nothing was witnessed around our unit. I wasn't particularly looking for it. With few exceptions, the hooch maids were older and not real attractive to American guys with American standards. After a while some guys weren't too picky though it seemed! We did have a cute girl working in our officers' club where I was club officer. Her name was Tue. Pronounced *Too - E.* She came and went every day on the base schedule, cleaned the club, washed dishes and glasses, and helped serve snacks and drinks. My roommate, Dick, became "involved" with her, let's say, to keep it civil.

There were some really nice Vietnamese people who came to work every day in our unit, and I took the opportunity to get better acquainted with them whenever possible. I was very interested in getting to know the average Vietnamese better, how they lived, and what they thought of us. It was fun trying to talk with them. For the most part, they appeared to be a polite, smiling, and happy people.

We also knew that we had VC on base during the day. They looked like every other Vietnamese. The MP's (Military Police) and others would occasionally catch them mapping out our flight line or attempting to do other things to try to damage or hurt us somehow. This was a guerrilla war after all.

One of my first real flights was as copilot flying a D model Huey troop lift helicopter. All new pilots in Vietnam flew as copilot for a couple weeks to get acquainted with the flying routines and missions. Our mission was to deliver a hot lunch to the ground troops in this one area of jungle. We were loaded down with thermite cans, large high efficiency thermos type cans that transported hot food. A hot meal in the boonies was a treat occasionally given to ground troops. We approached our landing site identified with a green smoke grenade and came to a fast landing in a small opening in the jungle. It was reported to be a *hot* area. Charlie was in the area and the troops were generally engaging him wherever he could be found. Some troops ran out of their cover in the jungle to the clearing bent over at the waist as they came under our rotor blades. They grabbed the cans of food and ran back into the jungle. It took only a few seconds. We took off out of there and climbed to an altitude of around 3,000 feet as fast as we could, which was pretty fast. We didn't get shot at but I probably wouldn't have known at that point, since I hadn't had that experience yet. We returned to base and that was our work for the day, about a three hour flight in total.

My next flight was the following day on a lift ship again as copilot. Our mission was to carry Vietnamese combat troops in a formation flight of five helicopters, and land them in an LZ (landing zone) near some action with Charlie. We were the third ship back from the lead ship, on the right side of the flight formation, and we were going to land the troops in a reportedly hot LZ. Landing in a hot LZ involved touching down on the ground in an area where there was ongoing enemy activity, expecting we might get shot at. We were not to be disappointed!

As we neared touchdown in our landing area, we came under heavy and continuous automatic weapons fire from the right side, from off in the jungle. As copilot, sitting on the right side in the cockpit, I was directly in the line of fire. I looked out to the right and saw the muzzle flashes. Not a desired place to be. A sitting duck, and they were shooting at me! I was not flying at this point, just sitting, backing up the pilot in command and along for the experience. And I was getting some, free of charge. I sort of hunkered down in my seat, without wanting to be too obvious, behind the armored plate that slid out from the right side of my seat. One can't get too small in this situation.

Looking to the right, I could see this one guy shooting at our flight of helicopters and the ground troops from about 100 yards away on the edge of the jungle. Our door gunners were firing their machine guns continuously into the jungle, and the ground troops were also firing their weapons as they got out of the helicopters. It was a wild, exciting scene. The seconds seemed to drag by in slow motion. I looked forward ready to take control of the helicopter if needed, watching the ships ahead of us, ready to take off in formation. I could see enemy tracer bullets zipping by between us and the helicopter about fifty feet ahead of us. I held my breath half expecting to be hit at any moment. I began to experience a special kind of feeling in my bowels. It was hard to know if I was shitting my pants or sucking the seat up. It was an unusual and not real pleasant feeling. This was to become the very definition of *pucker factor* for me.

Some troops didn't want to get off the helicopters and were kicked off by their commanders, or our flight crew, and others were shot just as they got off and fell in the mud. We didn't stay on the ground long, only a few seconds while the troops jumped out, then we quickly took off in formation. All of the helicopters took off out of the LZ, and some had bullet hits.

We took off as fast as possible, but only made a few hundred feet of altitude before we were hit by enemy fire. *In Vietnam two weeks and experiencing that special sound and feel of bullets ripping through my helicopter makes a person sit up and take notice. And still a new guy.* We were hit several times. The helicopter taking off behind us called right away and reported that we were on fire. We reportedly were trailing a lot of smoke. As we were only about three hundred feet above the ground, our pilot in command immediately looked for a landing site in the surrounding jungle and we started down. The helicopter was still flying okay, but it's not a good thing being on fire in any sort of flying machine, especially with a thousand pounds of fuel on board.

We made a hasty landing in a small muddy patch of ground with jungle all around. We all jumped out and prepared to get away as quickly as possible. We were very near the guys who shot us down and were concerned they might sneak up and try to finish the job. I drew my trusty S&W .38 and watched the bushes. I was totally exposed standing up out in the open. While watching the bushes, I grabbed my flight helmet bag, maps, and communication radios from the front of the helicopter. We all gathered up anything off the helicopter that might be useful to the enemy. Fortunately, another helicopter from our flight was on the way in to pick us up.

We looked at our helicopter quickly in the few seconds that we were on the ground and noticed that what was left of our fuel was draining out the bottom. We were not on fire. As it turned out the bullets we took ripped out much of the bottom of our fuel tank, and as our fuel was dumping overboard it had been vaporizing into the slipstream behind us as we were flying. It looked like smoke to the guys flying behind. Why all that jet fuel vaporizing into the air didn't catch on fire or explode behind our 450 degree centigrade jet engine exhaust is still a mystery. It's good to be lucky sometimes.

Ironically, the biggest downside to the whole experience for me was that in the rush to get out of the area where we'd gone down, the book I was reading was left behind and never returned. It was a Zane Gray western novel. It was not very good anyway so I guess it was no great loss. We were flown back to base, got in another helicopter, flew back out and rejoined our flight. The balance of the day is a blank in my memory. Funny thing. Enough excitement for one day.

Our base at Dong Tam was on the Mekong River and a navy base was located on the shoreline. A navy ship, the *U.S.S. Benewah*, an APB 35, which was a fairly large command ship of the navy's mobile riverine force, was anchored in the river. Many of our munitions and other supplies were brought in by LST, a different ship, upriver from Vung Tau. The navy had conducted mobile riverine combat operations all over the Mekong Delta against the Viet Cong, beginning in the early to mid-1960s. Later in the 1960s, the army became more heavily involved in the Mekong Delta with air mobile helicopter operations. Helicopters could go anywhere, faster, without being confined to rivers and canals. The enemy could be pursued more effectively. We also flew in support of continuing navy operations on occasion.

One bright, sunny day I flew single ship in the local area, simply providing support to navy operations. We flew out to the *Benewah* and landed high up on the fantail, the back of the ship, on a helicopter pad that was about thirty feet square. This was really interesting, being something new to me. We picked up someone and took him onto base. Later that day we flew out to a smaller river nearby and landed on a small, motorized barge that was anchored to the shoreline. The landing area on the barge was very small. We landed exactly on the "X" marked on the helicopter pad mid ship. We shut down to wait. As our rotor blades slowed down to a stop we saw that our rotor blades were clearing a pilothouse on the left by about one foot, and on the other side cleared some large antennas also by about a foot. We had to be real careful and precise at times in our flying. I would fly more for the navy in the months ahead providing gun cover.

Working with the navy was always great duty and we didn't get shot at much.

Flying many more times in lift ships over the next several days, I was able to gain more experience including a lot more combat action. It was fun for the most part, flying in a beautiful, warm, sunny country with water and palm trees all around. For a young guy who had invested a lot of time and effort in training learning to fly in a combat environment, it was thrilling, but was also quite risky at times.

CHAPTER 6

GUN PLATOON AND THE COBRA

Around the first of March, I was transferred to the gun platoon where the primary mission was to provide gun cover in C model Huey gunships to the troop lift operations flown by the lift platoon. We also flew several other types of missions such as close air support to ground troops, special air to ground rocket strikes on designated targets, high speed, low level raids on known enemy positions, convoy cover for truck convoys out of Saigon and flying cover for navy river operations up and down the rivers and canals near us. Fun work, usually.

One early mission flown as copilot was a raid about fifty clicks (kilometers) west of base. The images of it are still vivid. Our intelligence people reported that a small area of jungle off to the west was a Viet Cong communications and weapons relay location. The mission was to hit the location fast and hard from low level, and kill everything living that we found. We did our map study, planned the mission and route of flight, had a mission briefing with our wingmen and took off. It would be about a half hour flight to the target. The destination was a free fire zone, meaning we could shoot anything and everything without getting permission first.

We arrived on target at about 150 miles an hour, right on the treetops, and achieved total surprise. The area was near a canal, and the areas around a couple of hooches were covered with a few feet of standing water. Although people started running for cover, some were left caught out in the open. As three people were hurrying to get through the water to take cover, I shot one guy with our 40 mm cannon. He was blown in half, and his legs and lower torso ended up floating on the water. I didn't see the rest of him. Another guy was shot by one of our door gunners and fell into the water. A woman hurried over through the water, grabbed him and began to pull him away. We hovered over close and our door gunner shot her. They both lay motionless in the water. There were a couple other kills as well. A few pigs and a water buffalo that would be useful to the VC were also shot. The chickens were too small and too fast to hit. Mission complete. All of this only took ten minutes or so.

As we were heading back to base, still in the free fire zone, we came across a lone guy walking across the middle of a large open dry rice paddy. He had his shirt off and it was rolled up under his right arm. It appeared that he could be carrying something wrapped up in his shirt like a mortar, some sort of explosive, ammunition, or other item. We flew down low to a hover and circled around him to take a closer look. He kept on walking. We decided to take him out, so to speak. Our door gunners opened up on him with their machine guns at close range, no more than fifty feet away. The guy took several bullet hits and kept on walking, but was slowing down. He dropped his shirt. There was nothing in it. Our door gunners continued firing. The guy's left arm fell limp at his side and was totally red with blood running down dripping off his fingers onto the ground. A few seconds later he fell to the ground and started to crawl, clawing his way along with his one good arm. Our door gunners shot him some more, and he finally stopped moving. It's amazing how tough a human body can be. One of our door gunners wanted to shoot the guy some more with a pistol and take some pictures, so we hovered around a couple more times. I was still a new guy flying gunships and was just riding along as copilot. This experience left a real impression on me. Recalling this action many times over the years, it still upsets me a little. Combat can be a nasty sport.

The details of this day are still vivid after all these years. The sights are seared into my memory. I didn't feel real good about it, but we performed the mission. This was fairly typical action for gunship pilots and I knew many similar experiences lay ahead.

Our unit was due to have our old C model Huey gunships replaced with new Cobra helicopters over the next few months. The Cobra was the newest high performance helicopter gunship in the military. The marines were flying them also. It was a real widow maker though; it had to be flown right or else.

My orders soon came to attend in-country Cobra School at Vung Tau, a multiservice base 150 miles east of Dong Tam, on the South China Sea. I was probably selected as the first gun pilot from our unit to go to Cobra School because I was becoming recognized as a good pilot, had done well in flight school, and had been through the special helicopter gunship course. It would be an almost month long vacation, of sorts, especially compared to getting shot at.

Cobra School was five days a week, either in a classroom or out flying the Cobra. We had weekends off which was a real treat. A little guilt was felt being away from my buddies who were left back at home base exposed to daily combat action. I lived in a small, old French villa just off base on the edge of town. Vung Tau had a population of about ten thousand people including Vietnamese civilians, American troops of all stripes, Australian troops, Korean troops, and by default because they were everywhere, some Viet Cong and North Vietnamese Army troops. Vung Tau was considered an in country R&R (rest and relaxation) area for allied troops. It also was a supply depot.

The town was divided with some VC and NVA presumed to be on the west side amongst the native population, and we allied folks on the east side. There were also a lot of Vietnamese civilians on our side. We were separated from the bad guys by a city block between two city streets that ran generally north and south, sort of a buffer zone. Our side was a larger area and we had the best beach, which was the most important thing! It was not safe to be on the west side at any time, so no one from the Allied side ever crossed over through the buffer zone. There was sort of an unofficial truce in the area. It was peaceful for the most part largely because both sides had to be cool and not stir up trouble, although there was a lot of gunfire at night from the west side. Maybe the bad guys were getting training in how to aim and shoot a gun. At us! Many Viet Cong and NVA that we engaged in the boonies were pretty bad shots. Some were good enough though.

The villa where I lived was a great experience. It was a place that could have been right out of some European village It would be a great treat to go back now and vacation for while or spend a winter there. It had a high stone wall with broken chards of glass in a cement cap surrounding the compound for security. There was only one way in and out through a main gate with armed guards on duty around the clock. The building was four stories high with each floor twelve feet high or so. It was open and airy.

My room was on the first floor at the end of a hall, away from the large open-air main entrance. There was one window in the room with steel bars on it, but no glass. It was right next to one of the stone walls around the compound. It didn't feel real secure since a grenade could have been lobbed over the wall near or through my window, which was of mild concern. There was no air conditioning of course. There were two large ceiling fans called paddle fans hanging down from the twelve foot high ceiling that produced the only breeze. The fans were large with four or five foot long blades and turned very slowly. I was usually gone during the day, but the nights were quite humid and stuffy.

Gecko lizards would run all over the walls and ceiling at night, in the dark, cackling at each other. It took a few nights of watching carefully to finally figure out what was going on. I'd flip on the light and nothing could be seen. It seemed as though my eyes were playing tricks on me in the dark. They were fast little buggers. It was my first experience with this interesting lizard. They ate mosquitoes so they were good to have around.

The combination bathroom was in one small room in the corner of the main room, and was about three feet by five feet in size. There was a john at the end away from the door with a small sink and mirror on the left side. The shower was the whole room, spraying over the john and sink. An arm with a showerhead on it swung out from the wall on the right side into the middle of the room with hot and cold water controls in the wall. There was a central drain in the middle of the floor. It was a very efficient small space, and you never needed to clean the john, since everything got washed down whenever you showered. It was like having the john and sink in the shower. It was an interesting layout.

I had this room to myself. Actually there was another Cobra pilot trainee assigned as a roommate. I don't remember his name. After just one night he told me that he had found *a sweet little Vietnamese girl* to live with downtown. His girl was no doubt sweet and they were all little. Most likely, she was a *business* woman who probably got paid pretty well. The Vietnamese made their livings in all sort of ways. There were plenty of that type of business women around in most places in

Vietnam. So, although I saw my roommate every day in school, he never showed up in our room again. It was good though, I had the whole place to myself.

Our villa had an open air veranda on the third floor that served as our exclusive restaurant and bar. It was cool and airy in the late evenings, and was a welcome retreat after a day on the base airfield. The veranda was on a corner of the building overlooking a busy street intersection of town. There were no traffic lights, and no stop, yield or other types of signs. It was literally every person and vehicle for himself. It was entertaining. All sorts of vehicles crossed there continuously from all directions: trucks, jeeps, old 56 Chevys, European cars, donkey carts, hand drawn carts, motorcycles, bicycles, and cyclos. And people ran across the streets as they could. There was at least one significant collision every evening. Most injuries were minor, I think, although some people were dragged off to the edge of the street. It was really nuts and cheap entertainment.

In a city like Vung Tau most of the streets were busy with all sorts of vehicles and a lot of people walking around, including GI's. GI's often wore nice watches on display on their wrists. Nice watches were almost considered currency by the Vietnamese. Remember the scene in a movie or on TV where an Asian guy on the black market pulls up his sleeve and has a dozen watches on his arm that he's trying to sell? We had those guys here. There was an active black market in Vung Tau as there was in most other cities, and the Vietnamese were crafty thieves. Occasionally a pair of Vietnamese guys would ride by on a motorcycle close to some unsuspecting GI with a nice watch and hook on to it with a metal hook that they'd made, snap the watchband and take off with the watch. This had reportedly happened a few times. One guy was really upset when he lost his expensive Rolex that he had bought in Japan. But there was nothing you could do if you got robbed this way, except cry in your beer, which was what this guy was doing at the bar.

Next to our villa was a house occupied by two older American civilians from Washington State. They were Mom and Pop Warren. I discovered them one day when out walking around seeing the sights. They were missionaries, or something, with some volunteer organization who maintained an open house for American and Allied soldiers of any branch of the service, of any rank, from any country. Talk about supporting the troops. Stopping by to visit them, I was offered a standing invitation to dinner every evening at six o'clock. They didn't charge anything but would accept donations. They had a large dinner table and several guys were there for dinner each evening from different military services, US, Australia, and maybe other countries. A couple of guys even rented rooms from Mom and Pop. I ate there often and contributed a few bucks to support their activity. It was a nice experience. My first taste of mangos and papayas was there. The local fruit was delicious. We didn't ever get any fresh fruit in our mess hall at Dong Tam. Just canned.

One time when Pop Warren was headed into town to gas-up their Chevy van, he invited me along. We ended up at a Shell station of all things. Imagine a Chevy van at a Shell station, with the usual big yellow sign, in this old Vietnamese town. It was a bizarre experience. The ride in the Chevy was great. Pop paid with cash. What else? No credit cards here.

Vung Tau was really interesting. It was busy with local people coming and going every which way. It was hot, smelly and dirty, but fascinating. The normal taxi was a donkey or horse drawn cart. There were few cars. The taxi drivers would yell and cuss at the donkey or horse in English then turn around and laugh. Cuss words were probably the only English they'd learned. They wanted to humor us and make the ride entertaining so they would get a bigger tip. I didn't ride with them often. I did not want to go through that intersection near our villa! You can imagine how the streets smelled. It wasn't kept up like Mackinac Island that's for sure. It was hot and steamy. And you really had to watch your step. Donkeys were not the only animals to poop in the street.

Meat vendors sold raw, apparently freshly butchered meat on the street. At least it was red. They had carts that were maybe six feet long by three feet wide, with fairly large wheels on one end and legs on the other end where there was a handle to lift up and push the cart. Around the top of the cart was a wooden rack, the same size as the cart, about three feet high that was supported by posts at each corner. There were nails sticking out all the way around the rack where chunks of meat hung. They would push the cart along the street with the chunks of meat swinging from above. There was meat stacked on the cart as well. The vendor would push his cart along, yelling out his sales pitch to get people's attention. He didn't really have to say anything though. The thick cloud of black flies following the cart spoke with a loud voice and pretty much advertised what he was selling. We never got fresh meat in our mess hall, maybe for good reason. The meat looked pretty good actually.

One evening I went downtown with a fellow Cobra jock to sample some of the local cuisine. That fresh meat was just too tempting. We went into this fairly nice looking little café off one of the main streets for an evening meal. There was a U-shaped counter that pretty much occupied the whole restaurant where we sat on stools. I ordered the best steak dinner on the menu, not having a clue what sort of fare it might be. We probably ordered a beer or tea while we waited. There was no salad or other snacks available. The main dish came out a while later and looked pretty good. It was served on a large platter that was about the size of one of our meat serving platters. It was covered with a bed of white rice about half an inch thick. On top of the rice was a large cut of meat of some kind, probably water buffalo, which was thinly sliced to about a quarter inch thick. It had been pan fried. On top of the steak there were two fried eggs sunny side up. On top of the whole platter were some herbs and spices of some kind. There were some sauces in bottles on the counter that we could add if we wanted. It was really a great meal, different and quite tasty. I will always remember that café and the food. It would be great to go back there today, but the town certainly is not the same. There could well be a high rise there by now.

One weekend afternoon, I was walking downtown with a major and another captain, taking in the sights and smells. At one point an old lady walked off to the side of the busy street next to a tree, with people walking all around, dropped her pants and took a pee. *You don't see that in Kalamazoo too often.* We went into a teahouse to get a beer. It was a nice looking café right off a main sidewalk. We sat down at a low table with several chairs around and ordered beers. Soon a couple of pretty Vietnamese girls came over, sat down and asked us to buy them tea. They said, "You buy me tea?" with a heavy accent. We bought them glasses of hot tea that they likely considered expensive, but we considered very reasonable. This is how they got paid for socializing with us. It was always fun trying to communicate with Vietnamese, they with their limited English, and we with our limited Vietnamese. Every few minutes, while we sat there sipping our drinks and talking, another girl would come down a hallway toward us from a back room, stand in front of us, and open her brightly colored robe for a couple of seconds. She was wearing flip flops and a smile! They definitely understood the value of advertising. It seems there was more business conducted there than just selling tea. *Surprise, surprise!* None of us went to the back room although the invitation was very clear. Live floor models can be an effective form of advertising.

After a while, I walked up to a small counter off to the side of the front room where we were seated to where the apparent owner was standing. She was a nice looking older lady. I struck up a conversation with her, curious about who she was and what she thought about what was going on in her country. She poured me tea and poured herself some. We drank tea together and had a nice conversation. Her English was fairly good. She didn't charge me for my tea. It turned out she was from North Vietnam. It seems that in the very late fifties, as the French were moving out and the United States was beginning to move in with advisors, she decided she wanted to get away from communism and get closer to the kind of life that South Vietnam might offer. She made her way south on foot over a one-year period and arrived in Saigon. She then went farther on to Vung Tau, where we were now. We talked about a lot of things. She was very supportive of Americans in her country and did not like communism. *What else would one expect her to say?* It was an interesting conversation and a nice experience. She had a pretty young daughter that stuck right close to her. She appeared to be part French or American.

Later, while walking down the street, a young boy walked right up to the major I was with, stuck a magazine in his face and said, "You buy?" He was pretending to sell the magazine, but as he stuck the paper in the major's face, he reached under the magazine and grabbed a gold pen the major had in his shirt pocket. We grabbed his arm, took the pen back and sent him on his way with a kick in the butt. Another young boy came up to us and tried to sell his sister. Military people were the source of a lot of money.

Cobra school was a real flying experience. The Cobra is a high speed, high performance helicopter that was designed to be a very specialized aerial weapons delivery platform, a flying gun, from which different weapons can be fired at targets on the ground. We carried 7.62mm mini guns in a couple of different configurations, 40mm cannon, and the 3.75 folding fin aerial rocket, the same rocket that the air force used on their jets. Some Cobra's carried 20 millimeter cannon. The Cobra had a maximum air speed of 190 knots, about 240 miles per hour. It was the fastest helicopter around at the time. The flight controls fed into a computerized control system, a stability augmentation system called SAS, that helped stabilize the helicopter in flight and automatically provided a more stable airframe platform when firing weapons with the different recoil forces.

The Cobra was very sensitive and responsive in flight and it had to be flown carefully, paying special attention to some peculiar characteristics. For example, whenever maneuvered aggressively or pulled out of a dive, the rotor system tended to build rpm and could quickly over-speed if the pilot wasn't on top of what was happening. The lift control on the left side of the seat, the collective, had to be pulled up adding more pitch to the rotor blades to keep the rotor speed down in the proper operating range. The rotor system could be damaged with a rotor blade over-speed. The helicopter also sat high on narrow skids. It had to be set down carefully when landing to avoid tipping over sideways. I saw this happen one time about thirty paces in front of me. It was a great helicopter to fly and was challenging.

A situation occurred one time in Cobra school that nearly resulted in what would have been a serious crash. My instructor and I were flying out to a training field twenty miles or so north of Vung Tau by ourselves, into *no man's land*. There were no other helicopters with us, which was risky. If we crashed for some reason, no one back on base would be aware of it until much later when we failed to return. Radios weren't always manned very well, although we certainly would have made a distress call if there was time. The training field was a long open grass runway and, as we flew in the first time, I noticed a lot of broken up helicopter parts scattered along both sides of the landing strip that had been pushed back into the bushes. It made one pay extra close attention to his flying.

My instructor pilot was going to demonstrate a low level, high speed, down wind, engine failure, a technique involving a pop up, 180 degree, autorotation. There was always a lot going on with this maneuver. We flew down wind, or with the wind, on the tree tops at 180 miles per hour and my instructor rolled the throttle off, down to idle. This disconnected the engine drive from the rotor system simulating an engine failure. The rotor system was simply freewheeling at this point, like a spinning top. He pulled back on the cyclic control stick into a cyclic climb, which caused us to gain altitude rapidly using our speed and momentum. We climbed to an altitude of about 1,000 feet. With greatly reduced airspeed, around 40 miles per hour, and at around 1,000 feet, he made a right hand 180 degree turn back into the wind. Pilots always want to land their flying machines into the wind, since this minimizes ground speed at touch down. At this point, at the top of our climb and making a steep turn our rotor speed was dropping below operating range, which was normal. Keep in mind that our rotor is still freewheeling. As we began to fall like a rock down to a desired landing area, we leveled off and held our airspeed at around 80 miles per hour, according to published procedure. As we descended, our rotor speed was supposed to build back up into the proper operating range. Our rotor speed was low and we watched, waiting for it to increase. We would normally descend to around 100 feet above the ground, and then pull the nose up in a flare to reduce our descent and to slow our forward airspeed. We would then further settle toward the ground, with the rotor system still freewheeling, pull collective pitch, and softly touch down on the ground.

The problem this time was that our rotor speed was low because of the way the instructor had maneuvered through the whole process, and it did not build up the way it was supposed to on the way down. The instructor was doing all he could to try to get our rotor speed back. When we got near the ground where we needed to flare, the nose would not come up because of the low rotor speed. The more he tried to flare, the more rotor speed we lost. I was sitting in the front seat that was only about three feet from the nose of the Cobra. It appeared to me that we were going to hit the ground nose low. The ground was coming up fast and we could not get the nose up enough to slow down and touch down softly at near zero ground speed. Our speed was still around fifty miles per hour. In the last few seconds the instructor applied full throttle giving full power back to the rotor system. We regained some rotor speed and he kept us from hitting the ground. But it was close.

During those last few seconds near the ground, I had reached down and locked my shoulder harness. I thought the nose of the Cobra was going to impact the ground and we would cartwheel over forward. That would not have been a pretty scene. We probably would not have survived it. The helicopter would have shattered into pieces, our fuel tank would have ruptured and we most likely would have burst into a totally consuming fire. All helicopters tend to burn in a crash.

Anyway, we were near the end of our training day, so we flew back to base, not trying any more crazy stuff on the way. It was another good day, we were able to fly home. Any landing you can walk away from is a good landing, they say. *Back to work tomorrow.* I went back to my villa, cleaned up with a shower, *maybe rinsed out my shorts*, and went up to the third floor patio to eat, have a beer, and watch the crashes at the intersection. Great fun.

We also had training in firing all the weapons systems on the Cobra. Out on a firing range we fired rockets from the usual rocket pods, mini-guns in two different configurations; the flex mini-guns and mini-guns in stationary pods hard mounted on the stubby wings, and 40 millimeter cannon. The weapons systems were about the same that we fired from our older C Model Huey gunships. It was great fun firing the weapons from that sleek, fast helicopter.

One weekend we went to the beach on the South China Sea. Except for the overall environment surrounding Vung Tau, it was almost a tropical paradise. It was a hot sunny day with warm clean ocean water, white sand, and a gentle breeze. There were a couple of clapboard beach houses where we changed into swimsuits. Otherwise we were in our military duds which was normal dress. We had a nice time swimming in the ocean and spending some time on the beach, but it wasn't very relaxing. Lying on the beach in the sun, without a care, just didn't happen. It might have helped if my wife had been there with me. There were several guys up and down the beach and in the ocean with Vietnamese girlfriends. They were probably having more fun. The setting was real nice, but somehow didn't fit into the overall environment. Maybe it was just me. There was a large rusting freighter off a point of land to the west that had run aground many years before. Later that afternoon, we changed back into our normal cloths and got a taxi back to our villa.

I went to the base officers' club a few times in the evening to eat, have a couple beers and see what activities were planned for the evening. There were a lot of officers there of all ranks, from military units around the world. Most were American, of course. One time after dinner a few of us went to the lounge area where there were low tables and couches. There were Vietnamese girls there, most of whom were attractively dressed in their colorful local dresses. A couple girls came over and sat next to us, and on our laps, and we talked as we bought them tea. The usual social activity. The girl sitting with me mentioned her Vietnamese name, which I don't remember. She said her name meant *big boobs* and we all laughed. Looking casually, but likely obviously, I could tell that the name was fitting.

There was an occasional stage show at the officers' club. A bunch of guys went one evening and listened to a supposedly famous Vietnamese lady singer. She was dressed beautifully in a long dress, a flower in her hair and sang a variety of songs, from Vietnamese to popular American tunes. She was quite good. The only song I remember was one that the large group of guys really got into and all sang along with, *I Wanna Go Home*. The evening was uneventful, as usual with gunfire from the Commie side. It felt almost like home, back in Dong Tam.

The rest of Cobra school continued with the usual activity on base and flying. I tested out of my classroom and flying work, got my completion certificate, and headed back to my unit at Dong Tam as a fully qualified Cobra pilot. As I was flying away the next morning across Vung Tau Bay, with a couple guys from Dong Tam who flew over to get me, I noticed a Chinook helicopter, the large twin rotor cargo lift helicopter, carrying a beautiful camouflage painted Helio Courier airplane hanging on a long strap below. While admiring the beautiful airplane, the Chinook pilot punched off (released) the airplane and it dropped almost straight down, crashing into the ocean. Apparently, it was being disposed of in an ocean dumping ground. It was a sad sight. I sure would like to have had that airplane back in the States. It must have had some bullet or other structural damage that was considered not repairable, so they simply disposed of it at sea. What a waste.

Arriving back in my unit at Dong Tam, I was *The Cobra Guy*. Our gun platoon was scheduled to have our older C model Huey gunships replaced with new Cobras. I was probably going to become the instructor pilot. A couple of different times over the next few weeks, we had six brand new Cobras marked for our unit and waiting for us at Vung Tau. Each time they were taken away from us and sent up north where the need was supposedly greater. It amounted to more military clout somewhere, no doubt. The First Cavalry assault helicopter units were located up north and they often got their way over units considered less important down south. Anyway, we never got Cobras over the remaining months of my tour. Maybe it was not meant to be, and maybe it was for the best. Making the change in our unit to flying the Cobra would have brought new challenges and new Cobra qualified gun pilots into my unit. We were getting along fine with our old beat up C model guns.

CHAPTER 7

BACK INTO ACTION

So, back into the action at my home at Dong Tam as a gunship pilot. And it took me no time to get back into shooting and getting shot at. Some life, huh?

About this time, the task of building a new officers' shower during my time off was given to me. I guess I had slipped up once and told someone that I had some building experience. The reason for needing a new shower was that one night an artillery battery on the other side of Dong Tam, firing over us into an area of jungle two or three miles away, hit our old shower, behind our BOQ, and blew it to bits. One of the rounds they fired was a *short round*, which was an artillery round that didn't shoot from the gun properly and landed short. A long way short in this instance. It came close to hitting our BOQ. *It's never good to hurt your own people with friendly fire!* Friendly fire incidents occurred all over Vietnam on a regular basis. It's one of the hazards in any combat environment.

After some time gathering up materials and supplies, a few volunteers pitched in and we built a much nicer shower in about a week. It was attached to our BOQ and had sinks, mirrors and running water, gravity fed from our water tower near by. It was really nice, comparatively speaking. The guys loved it.

An interesting thing happened one time with all our enlisted guys, which included our helicopter gunners and crew chiefs. The details aren't fully known, but as a group they had some kind of disagreement with their sergeants or officers who managed them. It may have had something to do with the duty roster and their work rotation. Anyway, they essentially went on strike as a group and refused to work. It involved seventy or eighty guys. In the military, people can't go on strike, but collectively, they can stop working. In this instance all our enlisted guys went on sick call. Our unit doctors supported their cause for some reason, giving them all sick passes, excusing them from work for the day. In this large a group the guys weren't worried about punishment. What was the boss going to do, send them to Vietnam?

This went on for two days. The missions still needed to be flown, so we did what had to be done. All pilots in our unit filled out the full crew requirement of two pilots and two door gunners. There were pilots sitting in the back of our gunships manning machine guns. A real scary situation! Some pilots had never held or pulled the trigger of the M60 machine gun. The missions we flew those two days didn't amount to much, thankfully. No one did much shooting. Some pilots had some fun with the machine gun though, shooting when they could. I flew one day and manned the machine gun in the back. It was unsettling just sitting in the back, having to trust some other pilot to do the flying. Any pilot feels better up front at the controls, in control. We made it through the two days without mishap, however. The enlisted guys got their issues resolved and went back to work. It was an interesting change of routine.

Flying gunships an average of four days a week, on a variable schedule, was fascinating. I flew as copilot for another week was then advanced to PIC, Pilot in Command, in the gun platoon. I soon became Fire Team Lead, or the commander of the team of gunships on missions. The different types of missions we flew were challenging, and fun for the most part. There were almost no recognizable weekdays or weekends though. Every day was like the one before.

One of the most effective, and deadly weapons our gunships were equipped with, were mini-guns. It was a modern day gattling gun, much the same as the one developed in the later days of the Civil War. It had six barrels arranged in a circle, side by side, sixty degrees apart. All the barrels spun around on a motorized base that rotated the barrel assembly. The gun fired the standard NATO 7.62 millimeter bullet. We had two mini-guns, one mounted on each side of the helicopter. The barrels spun around fast. Our slow rate of fire was 2,000 shots a minute, and our high rate of fire was 4,000 shots per minute. This amounts to 33 shots per second, and 66 shots per second respectively. That's a lot of firepower, and we could fire both guns together doubling the rate of fire. We only fired this weapon for two or three seconds at a time so we wouldn't burn out the barrels. We often didn't need to fire it for long anyway. It would clean up a target in a hurry. The best way to describe the sound when we fired the mini-gun is that it sounded like a roaring lion. We had to be very careful and very specific where we aimed and fired this weapon. It was feared every bit as much as rockets by the enemy.

Most of the missions we flew were covering air mobile operations where our lift ships were landing, dropping off, or picking up ground troops. Early on in my tour we hauled mostly American troops, then later on we carried mainly Vietnamese troops. Our Vietnamese allies were interesting to watch, but we had to be especially careful when they were around because there were often VC among their ranks. Performance of Vietnamese units varied a lot in how they were disciplined and led. Some troops were gung-ho, jumping out of the helicopters even before they touched down, and charging a tree line yelling and screaming. Other units would wait for the helicopters to touch down, step off casually, get down behind a dike line for cover, sit down and eat their C rations. Maybe they felt it could be their last meal. C rations were often a better meal than they were used to, complete with dessert, cigarettes, and toilet paper. We passed out "C rats" to all the Vietnamese ground troops that we carried. It was supposed to help motivate them. The attitude seemed to be either, live and you get to eat, or eat now because you may not live. Many Vietnamese army troops were lazy it seemed and not very good.

A few of the door gunners and crew chiefs in our unit were shot in the feet. It occurred in our lift platoon. The gunners' feet often would be sticking out the side of the doors of the helicopter as they flew on missions and fired their M60 machine guns. They were wearing *chicken plates* (body armor) to protect their chests and sitting on extra chicken plates to protect their bottom sides. They were openly exposed to enemy fire all the time. As they were shooting their machine guns they were shooting all around the open door. They had to be very careful. And accidents happened. They would sometimes shoot their own helicopter in the rotor blades, doorframes, skids and other places. If the bad guys didn't get them first, some guys even shot their own feet, usually by accident. We found out though, that some guys who were especially afraid of getting wounded or killed, would sometimes intentionally shoot their own foot. It was an instant ticket home. They figured it was better than being killed. Some people can reason pretty well, and had some guts to go along with it. We had this happen four or five times in our unit during my year. Aircrew members intentionally shooting their own feet happened some all over Vietnam.

We were supporting ground troops one afternoon, south of our base at Dong Tam, across the Mekong River some thirty clicks or so. It was getting late and the sun was going down. We were in action with Viet Cong. As we were flying around supporting our troops and chasing VC, we got a low rotor speed warning and our main rotor tachometer needle dropped to zero. I knew right away that the tachometer had broken because our rotor was still spinning normally. It was not unusual to have things break, so we continued to fly the mission. A few minutes later another warning lit up on our instrument panel indicating that the EGT, exhaust gas temperature system, was malfunctioning. The temperature indication on the instrument panel was jumping all over the place, a gauge that is normally very steady. Initially the thought was that another part on the engine was simply failing, which again was not too unusual. These two indications took readings directly off physical electrical connections to the engine.

As I continued to fly around, it occurred to me that the chance that two systems would break so close together was very unusual. The failure of these two separate operational systems was sending a strong message that something more serious was probably going on behind us. The engine and helicopter were continuing to operate normally, however. I called our Command and Control, told our mission commander what was going on and requested permission to head back to Ben Tre, a small unsecured refuel and rearm airstrip some twenty clicks to our north. It would not be good to be on the ground with Charlie after dark.

We headed back to Ben Tre alone, a fifteen minute flight away, as it was getting dark. I climbed up to three thousand feet or so to get a little security at altitude as we flew north. If our engine quit, or we had other problems, we would have more time to call for help on our way down from higher altitude. A couple minutes into the flight our engine started to fail. Our engine was on automatic governor control, but our engine RPM would drop off, then build back up again on its own, out of control. Something was going on back there and it wasn't good. When our engine would apparently fail with a drop in engine and rotor speed, I would go into partial autorotation and begin going down. I called our C&C to keep him advised of our status. As we worked our way closer to our landing objective, our engine got worse. It would fail, come back on, then fail again. The cycle was becoming more frequent and we still had a few miles to fly. I was careful to keep our rotor blade rotational speed in normal operating range, for that's what would keep us flying.

As we got closer to the landing strip, I eased off on the power and began making a slow decent toward the airfield, while maintaining airspeed up around 100 knots in our glide. The engine was getting close to total failure now, but kept coming back on with partial power. In this type of situation you don't try to save the engine, you use what power you have to aid your descent and try to make a safe landing and let the engine self-destruct if need be. Maneuvering to line up with the runway, I slowed our airspeed as we made our approach to land. The engine was failing almost completely by now and if we made it to the runway we would not be able to hover above the ground as we slowed down. I decided to make a run-on emergency landing and skid along the runway to a stop much like an airplane would land. We came across the end of the runway doing about 80 knots, which was still fast. I slowed down more, got close to the runway surface and touched down skidding toward a full stop. Before we landed, I had called the crew on our intercom and told them to unbuckle their seat belts, jump out and get away from the helicopter as soon as we got slow enough I reached across and pulled my door jettison handle and kicked the door out. As we were skidding to a stop, I reached to the instrument console and switched off our fuel and turned off the battery switch. As soon as the helicopter came to a full stop I also jumped out and got away quickly. The fear was that the helicopter would catch fire.

There was no fire but fuel was pouring out of both sides of the engine compartment, down the sides of the helicopter and onto the ground. It could easily have caught on fire in flight or on the ground. We were lucky again.

We were picked up by one of our lift helicopters returning from the mission and taken back to base. *Home to supper!* It was another interesting day, not one that we thought much about afterwards. It happened, we got more in-flight emergency flying experience, and we were okay. Back to work the next day.

The aircraft was secured with ground troops overnight and recovered by our maintenance people the next day. We were always curious what the problem was when this sort of operational problem occurred. It turned out that our jet engine was slowly cracking in half around the fuel annulus where fuel was injected into the engine and the combustion chamber. It was a structural failure of the engine which was quite unusual. *Trash another one.*

Another day, we were supporting some American ground troops, just south of Dong Tam across the Mekong River, in an area from which we were quite regularly mortared at night, sometimes even during the day. The VC mortars would not fly very far, so they had to get within a mile or so of their target. Our ground troops were working this area to try to clear it of people that fired the mortars and maybe teach the locals a lesson. We were flying around low looking for VC they might flush out. As our troops were working their way through one area of jungle, several people walked out ahead of them. They walked into an open rice paddy where there was no cover, no place to hide. VC often would do this, to appear like locals, and be able to simply walk away without being attacked. In this instance it was a big mistake. Our commander, overhead in the command and control ship, told us to engage them. In other words, to kill them. So we maneuvered into position and opened fire. The people started scattering in all directions. One guy dove into a small canal running along the rice paddy trying to hide under the edge, but the water was quite clear and we could still see him. I was flying in the copilot seat that day, manning the 40 mm cannon, technically called a grenade launcher, which was a flex weapon that fired the rounds wherever I aimed the sight. I put the sight on the bad guy and pulled the trigger. The rounds exploded on impact. The water turned red.

Next we went over to the open rice paddy where several of the "enemy" were running, trying to get away. But there was nowhere to go. I fired at one guy and had a direct hit. After the smoke cleared from the explosion, the guy was gone, he'd disappeared. The door gunners were also getting kills. It was not a pleasant scene. It was like shooting ducks on a pond. None of the people had weapons that were visible.

After what seemed like a long time, but was only a few minutes, it was over. The ground troops walked in and started mopping up. We continued to fly around the area covering the withdrawal of our ground troops. Between the ground troops and the gunships, there were many kills lying around. The ground commander called and gave us the number of kills that we could claim in our After Action Report. We recorded our kills each day with marks put on the edge of our windshield with a black grease pencil. The cumulative number of enemy killed every day, added up from all over Vietnam, was supposedly a measure of success in the Vietnam War. We reported our black marks.

After several minutes continuing to fly cover and finish up the operation, we flew over to a nearby road where a lot of people had gathered. There seemed to be a lot of activity and we were curious as to what was going on. A small dump truck was parked there and a couple of men were picking up bodies from a fairly large pile and throwing them into the back of the truck. There were several women standing around weeping hysterically. As I flew over and looked into the back of the truck, it reminded me of some of the pictures we have all seen of Jews stacked in pits, at concentration camps, at the end of World War II, only on a much, much smaller scale of course.

By this time I was not feeling too well, nor proud of what we had done, but nothing was said. We had followed orders. We had several black marks on our windshield. As we were flying around doing our work that day, it appeared to me that most of the so-called enemy were young people, perhaps teenagers. They could well have been the ones, however, that were transporting and assembling the mortars during the day that were fired at us at night, and quite possibly the ones doing the firing. Such was the nature of guerrilla war. Locals would appear to be friends by day and then be the enemy by night. Talk about being stuck between a rock and a hard place.

I didn't eat or sleep too well for a couple days, but the bad feeling passed. One toughens up mentally. I found this sort of experience to be quite sobering. It numbed the senses and emotions. I didn't keep count, but my number of kills was growing.

In most areas on military bases and out in the boonies, Americans and Vietnamese both constructed bunkers of various types to help protect themselves during military action. The U.S. military built bunkers to go to during mortar or rocket attacks and guards occupied bunkers while protecting a base perimeter. Some American troops out in the boonies lived in bunkers. Americans would build bunkers out of steel drums filled with dirt, heavy wood timbers, PSP planking, sand bags, dirt, steel roadway drainage tiles, and anything else they could get their hands on.

The Vietnamese also built bunkers. Some were in towns and villages and some were out in the boonies near open rice paddies. The Vietnamese out in the boonies would build their bunkers out of anything they could find. Their bunkers were often made by forming a small dome out of wood, tree limbs, metal sheets, and such, then covering it in layers of mud and straw. They would add layers of mud and straw until the top and walls were perhaps three feet thick. It would bake hard in the sun. The space inside might be very small and hold only three or four people, while the outside was perhaps ten feet across and ten feet high. There was a small access door that could be closed. They looked almost like igloos, but brown instead of white. Many times we would see VC, or suspected VC, run into bunkers ahead of us as we flew into an area. Sometimes we'd shoot our rockets at bunkers, and other times we would wait for the ground troops to flush people out. Bunkers were important protection for locals who lived out in the boonies.

Once, I flew a larger D model Huey for our unit commander on air-mobile command and control operations for the day. Early in the morning we flew into My Tho, the small village near our base at Dong Tam, and landed near the U.S. military compound. Our landing site was near the center of this interesting old town. *What inviting little village, it would have been great to have lived there.* We picked up an American ground commander, a colonel, and a Vietnamese official of some sort. The colonel was the overall commander of the ground troops out on operation that day. Our lift helicopters carried his troops, then landed them in a designated landing zone where they worked the area looking for Charlie. I sat in that pilot's seat flying for fourteen hours straight. I got out of the helicopter only twice, while on the ground for refueling or to step a few paces away and take a pee. The ground commander brought a box of sandwiches to eat and we bought some bananas from some local kids. Bananas were good since they were easy to eat and they were filling. The long day was completed without too much trouble. Returning late, it was good to get back to my hooch.

As Pilot in Command (PIC) of my gunship, I began leading and commanding gunship missions. There were normally one or two other gunships flying behind me as my wingmen. We conducted our missions as a team. We were named Copperheads and my call sign was Copperhead 35. We called ourselves "snakes". At the end of the day we would fly home and park the gunships on the airfield, in our assigned parking area that we named the "snake pit". We had special colorful patches hand stitched by the local Vietnamese that we sewed on our flight suits that identified us as The Copperheads. We were generally regarded as armed and dangerous dudes. We made the whole experience as much fun as possible. *Ya gotta have some fun somehow!*

We flew the C Model Huey gunship, built by Bell Helicopter in Ft. Worth, Texas. It was sensitive, like most flying machines, especially if we took a bullet in a critical place. But it was also tough in a lot of ways, like a Mac truck. Our C Model gunships were considered more challenging to fly than other helicopters. Flying them required a more delicate touch and more skill in many circumstances. We had only a 950 shaft horse power jet turbine engine. The gunship was considered under powered considering all the weight we carried with fuel and munitions. As a result we often could not make a normal hovering take off and had to slide along the runway on our skids building up airspeed until we could lift off. We had to be real smooth on the controls. The more control movement we made the more power it required. It was normal procedure in the military that when a pilot crashed a helicopter, he would go before a flight review board to be evaluated for pilot proficiency, if he was still alive. When a pilot crashed a C model gunship there was no flight review board evaluation. Crashing a C model was not considered unusual, and the pilot was not held accountable due to the extra difficulty involved in flying it.

By now I had been given the nickname Wild Bill, specifically because I was very much the opposite. I had the reputation for staying calm, cool and level headed even in hot and heavy action when the bullets were flying. I was all business and very effective in my pilot and leadership role. My feeling was that if it was my appointed time to go, then I would go, and there would be little ability to change the outcome. With everything that was happening, we knew that we didn't have much control over outcomes other than doing our job the best that we could. So I just concentrated on my flying and doing my job, and didn't worry too much about the risks.

I scrounged up an additional personal weapon to carry with me when flying. My rusty trusty Smith & Wesson .38 revolver didn't amount to much actual protection. I was able to get an M3A1 tank commander's weapon. It was a small .45 caliber machine gun commonly called the *Grease Gun* because it indeed looked a lot like a grease gun. It didn't work quite right initially, but after several nights working on it in my hooch, I was able to analyze the function and fix it so it worked normally. It was test fired flying while my copilot took over the controls. It was a little extra personal protection if needed when we went down, or when sitting around between missions out in the boonies. One never knew where the bad guys were.

Another pilot from Louisiana, nicknamed Cajun, who flew with me a lot as my copilot, got a hold of a traditional Thompson submachine gun somewhere. This is the same machine gun made famous by Al Capone in Chicago, during Prohibition that we used to see in the Elliot Ness movies. The movies had it right, it was a real hot performer with a high rate of fire. It would spray the cockpit with empty hot brass cartridges whenever Cajun was firing from his copilot seat. The sleeves and collar on my flight suit were fastened tight around my wrists and neck to keep hot brass cartridges from going down my flight suit and burning me. The hot brass would bounce off our flight controls, the instrument panel, me, my helmet and face shield. He had two thirty-round clips of ammo taped together, side to side, so he had sixty rounds available before he had to reload. Quite often we would fly around low with our doors off, especially during the dry season, and Cajun would fire his Thompson out his open door as we flew around chasing Charlie. He had a lot of fun. It was exciting, especially when Charlie shot back at us. Crazy, huh?

Occasionally Cajun and I would be down, not flying, on the same days. We would sometimes go to our supply room and draw out bows and arrows, then set up a target on the side of our hooch and shoot arrows at the target. The bows and arrows were there for recreational activity. Given the nature of our work when we flew, this was almost funny. We got a lot of *recreational* activity when we flew. Shooting bows and arrows was a bit humorous at the time, but we killed some time and got some official recreation. Our unit also had horseshoes, of course.

Our Crew chief and gunner, on each side in the back of our gunships, had M60 machine guns. These fired the standard NATO 7.62mm ammunition. It was normal procedure for them to fire out the open cargo doorways at various targets. Given our mission, they did a lot of shooting. Shooting out the side of a flying aircraft of any kind was a special skill. We had a door gunner who flew with me a lot who was a really good shot. He had been in our unit for three years straight. He was making good money and had no reason to go home. One day we were supporting ground troops in the normal fashion, flying out ahead of them. There had been some action with Charlie. As we flew along a dike line, at an altitude of about three hundred feet, our gunner saw a suspected VC standing next to a tree. He aimed his machine gun and squeezed off a short three round burst of fire. The guy fell over. I was amazed. That was good shooting. Put another black mark on the windshield.

On occasion, depending on the type of missions we were to fly for the day, we would carry a wooden box full of hand grenades of various types on the floor, right behind the instrument console between our pilot seats. The grenades could be reached by either pilot and by both door gunners in the back. We often flew missions that required us to fly slowly at treetop level, scouting ahead of ground troops. We might be flying over tunnels or bunkers and would try to flush Charlie out. Doing most of the flying in these situations, I never played with grenades much, but the crew in the back would often pick a grenade, pull the pin, and throw it out the door at some target on the ground. I always cautioned my crew to be very, very careful. You can imagine why. A dropped grenade bouncing around in the back of the helicopter with the pin pulled would result in not such a good day. We would probably not be flying home.

Concussion grenades were often used and the explosion, and resulting concussion, were really intense. It would severely rattle the brains and disorient people nearby, which was the intent. We had to be flying away at a good speed to get away from this grenade after it was tossed out the door. Having live grenades on board was always a significant concern to me. It didn't give me a warm, fuzzy feeling. We got shot at and hit a lot, and one bullet in the crate of grenades right behind us would not have been a good deal. *Boom. Notify the folks back home.*

We also flew in tear gas at times, either from our own tear gas grenades or from the ground troops. Tear gas was frequently used around tunnels and bunkers. While circling overhead waiting for Charlie to come out, we would fly in the gas until we started choking and our eyes watered until we could hardly see. We would fly away for a few minutes, get some fresh air then go back in. Gas masks were issued, but they weren't practical to wear with a flight helmet and microphone, so we never used them.

One day we were flying missions to the south, fairly close to our base at Dong Tam. We were rotating back and forth to our home base for re-arming and refueling as necessary. On one rotation we parked at re-arming so our crew could get out to reload rockets and the 40 mm cannon. The helicopter was still running at flight idle, so I stayed on the flight controls, which was normal procedure. The 40mm cannon was mounted on the nose of the helicopter. It was an electric motor powered mechanical firing weapon. Procedure for the gunner, upon landing, was to immediately go to the 40mm, on the nose, and safe the weapon by spinning the firing mechanism backward, unloading the weapon. Spinning the firing mechanism forward cycling a round through the weapon would sometimes cause the cannon to fire off a round accidentally. The gunner was standing off to the side of the weapon as he was supposed to, not in front of the barrel, which was a good thing, because he rotated the firing mechanism the wrong direction and the 40mm fired off a round.

I had made one simple mistake in the whole procedure in our rush to rearm and get back into the action. I had parked the gunship, and the 40mm, pointed directly at a guard tower on the corner of our airfield. The 40mm projectile was slow and you could see it go out through the air. It looked like a black golf ball driven off the tee. When the cannon fired, the round headed right at the guard tower with two guys in it. *Oh s--t!* I held my breath. Luckily the round went over the roof of the tower, clearing it by about one foot. I started breathing again. *Whew!* The cannon round continued to fly out past our base perimeter and blew up in an open rice paddy. The sirens went off on base signaling a mortar attack. *Little did they know!*

We finished our loading, quickly, and took off flying away, back to our mission. Nothing became of this near miss accident.

We and the guys in the guard tower were fortunate. It's not good to shoot your own people. I tried to be more mindful of where we pointed our weapons after that experience. It was a challenge to remember everything all the time, but it was a good thing to try and do.

Command detonated mines, IED's in today's lingo, were used at every opportunity by the Viet Cong and NVA. They would often use our own artillery rounds that had been shot into an area but did not explode on impact for some reason. Charlie, or sympathetic locals, would go looking for dud rounds after an artillery strike and would sometimes find one. They would bury the still live explosives in rice paddies, in places where they figured our lift helicopters might fly in and land. They would attach an explosive on the artillery round, like a hand grenade, then run wires back into the edge of the jungle. Some VC, or other local, had the duty to camp there for as long as it took for a flight of helicopters to come in and land. He would pull the wire as the helicopters touched down, setting off the explosive, then run for his life. And he usually got away.

One time we were covering a flight into an open area, in a dry rice paddy, just south of the Mekong River. The memory is as fresh as yesterday. We were circling overhead watching the flight as they touched down, and *BOOM*. The second ship back had its tail blown off right behind the crew compartment by a mine. Soon we heard the report from our Command and Control. An American lieutenant was killed in the explosion as he was getting out of the helicopter. It was not the sort of thing one ever wants to hear. He was loaded on another one of our helicopters and flown back to our unit at the airfield. He was later unloaded and laid on the ground right outside our operations office. I was still flying so I didn't see him. He was picked up by the Graves and Registration people and taken to the cooler. He had reportedly had the back half of his head blown off. He certainly never felt a thing. It would be an okay way to go if your number was up.

Another day we were covering a flight of five lift helicopters from behind and alongside the flight. We were firing rockets around and below the flight, aiming up ahead of them as they were making their approach to a potentially hot LZ. We would often cover our lift ships' approach to an LZ like this since the bad guys would take cover from our rocket fire and not fire at the flight, as they landed. As our lift ships would slow down and land, we would circle around them and lay down suppressive fire as needed to protect them. On the way in to the LZ this time, I was flying behind and a little below the flight, firing rockets. One rocket malfunctioned after launching from the rocket tube, with one of the four folding fins not folding out properly. The rocket began to cork screw badly off target. I held my breath as the rocket headed up toward our unsuspecting flight, cork screwing nowhere near where it had been aimed. Fortunately, the rocket dropped before it entered our formation flight of lift ships, and landed a long way short. After that scare I would allow more room between our flights and my rockets. Shooting down one of our own helicopters was a real scary thought.

We would still fire rockets real close sometimes though, depending on how hot an LZ or PZ (pickup zone) was and how close Charlie was. One of our lift pilots got a Purple Heart one day from my rocket shrapnel. We went into a real hot LZ and were flying low and real close on the left side of the flight. We all were taking enemy fire from the left and ahead. I was firing rockets alongside and ahead of the flight into the edge of the jungle. It was a very small LZ. My rockets were impacting and exploding all around, fairly close to our lift ships. A piece of my shrapnel apparently went up in the air then came down into the rotor blades of one helicopter. A rotor blade must have hit a chunk of the hot metal kicking it down through the green house window on top, hitting the pilot on the cheek, as it fell in his lap. He picked it up and put it in his pocket. It drew blood while he was engaged in combat action in a war zone, so he technically was wounded and received a Purple Heart. Some said it was cheap but those were the standards.

Departing from that same LZ, one of our lift ships was hit by the continuing enemy fire. The bullet went up through the belly of his helicopter then through the engine deck, apparently severing the main fuel line to the engine. The pilot had an immediate engine failure. He brought the helicopter to a complete stop above the jungle that was maybe eighty feet high, then did a hovering autorotation straight down through the trees to the ground. The rotor blades disintegrated as they cut their way down through the jungle and the airframe was broken up, but they landed upright with a bump, without a fire. The guys on board were not seriously hurt. While guarding the jungle around them, they moved to an open area and were picked up by another helicopter.

Another day in the life of a combat helicopter pilot and crew. Go back to base, have dinner and write another letter home. Report to the wife and folks that we had another normal day and all was just fine.

CHAPTER 8

AN INTERESTING LIFE

By now I had had some good experience flying, shooting rockets, mini-guns, and 40 millimeter cannon, and was routinely commanding gunship missions four or five days a week. Most of our missions involved directly supporting ground troops. Maintaining direct radio contact with the ground commander, we coordinated our overall activity with him. We were often very much an integral part of their ground combat operations. *Great fun.*

Ground troops really loved us gunships. We were their eyes in the sky, and provided a lot of direct, close up fire support that offered great security to them. We were like a big brother, and they felt better when we were overhead. I had great empathy for our ground troops. They had a hard job often in uncomfortable, dangerous circumstances. Many times there would be an explosion up on the leading edge of a column of ground troops where the point man was leading the way through the jungle. Someone had set off a booby trap of some sort. One booby trap Charlie sometimes set up was called a ball buster. It was a hand grenade, that when triggered would pop up out of the ground and blow up about waist high. We often figured one of our guys had been wounded or killed when we heard the explosion from a booby trap. Walking around in the jungle was not a great place to be. We worked hard for the ground troops.

Many ground troops thought, however, that what we were doing was crazy. We were flying around slowly, often just above the tree tops, and were sitting ducks, with nowhere to hide from enemy fire. We could easily crash to the ground after being shot at and hit. That was a scary thought for a lot of ground troops and maybe most other sane individuals. At least they could jump into a foxhole or behind a tree to take cover. I was happy though to be doing some pretty exciting flying.

We usually flew real low on missions where we supported ground infantry units, so we were often in the action with them. Our two door gunners worked out with their M60 machine guns as necessary. We would fly out ahead of the troops scouting out an area conducting *recon-by-fire*. We would shoot weapons that best fit the conditions into areas where it was suspected that the enemy might be and try to get them to shoot back, giving away their position. We would fly in a position that made us a good target, inviting the bad guys to shoot at us. Sometimes the temptation was too great. When they shot at us, we would turn on them with our superior firepower, doing a lot of damage. We called this kind of work *snoop and poop*. We would go snooping for trouble and poop on the troublemakers. It was interesting to go exploring and see what we could stir up. It also helped the ground troops. It would often expose enemy positions sooner so the bad guys could be dealt with more effectively, with fewer friendly casualties. Whenever we got into direct action with Charlie, the ground troops would go in afterward to mop up. When they found our kills the commander would call on the radio and give our kills to us to record. More black marks on the windshield.

We had two types of officers in the Army in Vietnam, warrant officers and commissioned officers. Warrant officers were specialists in certain fields. In our unit most warrant officers were pilots and specialists in flying. Commissioned officers were leaders and commanders who were also pilots. As a First Lieutenant, I was a commissioned officer. Not all warrant officers, or commissioned officers were pilots, of course. In fact, few officers in the larger military were pilots, most performing in other roles on the ground. Most officers, especially commissioned officers, also had extra duty assignments. At Dong Tam, I was our officers' club officer, or club manager, when not flying.

We had a rather interesting officers' club. It was also our officers' bunker that we all went to during mortar attacks, which usually occurred at night. The enlisted guys had their own bunker. Our bunker was about thirty feet wide and forty feet long. It was built of 8x8, and 16x16 inch square timbers fastened together into the basic structure. The walls then were planked with two-inch thick timbers. There was an inner wall and an outer wall with four feet of dirt in between. There was six feet of dirt on top of the ceiling of the bunker then a corrugated steel roof over everything. It was a pretty stout structure that was built to take a direct hit from a 122 millimeter rocket, so we were told. We were never attacked with rockets while I was there, only mortars. Some mortars came close but the officers' club never took a direct hit.

During mortar attacks, sirens would go off on base and everyone was supposed to go to their bunker. When first arriving at Dong Tam, and for some time thereafter, when we came under a mortar attack, all the guys would stand outside listening to the mortars whistle overhead and cheer when Charlie missed hitting anything significant. He normally was aiming at the airfield, trying to hit helicopters that were fifty to one hundred yards from our BOQ. He would have been happy to hit us too, of course. Occasionally he would damage a helicopter or two, but he mostly just harassed us.

We could count on incoming mortars on Sunday evening during *Bonanza,* that was picked up on Armed Forces Television out of Saigon. My roommate scrounged up a TV for our hooch and made an antenna from coat hangers. He was an avionics and electrical technician you recall. Sometimes we just sat and watched TV and ignored the fireworks outside. We couldn't miss Bonanza!

One night we came under another mortar attack and a mortar landed in our compound, close to our BOQ. After that bit of excitement most of us went to the bunker. A few guys still just slept through it, figuring like most of us did, that when you're number was up it was up. Our commander wanted all the guys to go to the bunker during mortar attacks though and he asked for my help with the problem. So as Officers' Club Officer, I established a policy that during mortar attacks we had open bar which meant free drinks and snacks. *Drinks were otherwise really expensive, you understand, ten cents for a beer.* The guys then started going to the bunker/officers' club more often. We'd have some drinks, listen to music, and play darts. If the mortar attack was in the middle of the night most of the guys were sleepy-eyed, in bare feet or wearing sandals, and were in their underwear. We were a real professional looking bunch of professional pilots.

One afternoon I checked out a large flatbed 2 ½ ton truck from our motor pool to go pick up a pallet of beer from the Class VI on base, about a mile away from our officers' club. It was another beautiful day in paradise for the drive to the center of our main base. After paying for and having the pallet of beer loaded, I began heading back north toward our airfield. All of a sudden there was the characteristic swishing sound of a mortar flying overhead and the sirens began blaring. The mortar fire was coming from the south across the Mekong River and was headed north toward the airfield. I immediately stepped on the brake, stopped the truck near a small bunker beside the road, jumped out and ran to it.

Getting to the opening of the bunker, I looked in. It was packed full of Vietnamese faces with big round eyes staring out at me. There was no more room. I ran back to the truck, jumped in and took off with the accelerator flat on the floorboard, figuring that a moving target was the best option. It wouldn't have made any difference of course if my number was up, but it was exciting.

Driving along, another mortar came swishing close overhead. It hit a building just up ahead of me, exploding and blowing up the building. I continued along to the airfield as a couple more mortars landed on the right side of the road. Dirt and dust were rising up in the air from the explosions. One mortar had landed in the middle of a U-shaped motor pool with trucks parked around. Driving by, I noticed a mechanic in a white T-shirt get up off the ground, look around, dust himself off, pick up his wrench from the ground and climb back up on the truck he had apparently been working on. Dust was still blowing away in the wind. It appeared that he felt it was no big deal. The mortars missed him and there likely would not be a repeat performance in the same spot. *If your number's up, it's up, if it's not, it's not. Go back to work.*

One night I was assigned to overnight guard duty with another guy, in a bunker that was on top of a square storage building, next to the runway where we parked our helicopters. We had sandbag walls all around. We were armed with an M60 machine gun and an M79 grenade launcher both of which we were trained to use. There were several guard towers and bunkers around the airport that were manned every night to deal with any VC who might try to come on to the airfield to damage our helicopters. It was a long night just sitting there watching our sector of the airfield. We alternated duty with one keeping watch and other taking a break, when you lie back, relax and maybe get a little sleep.

One time I was taking a break lying on my back on top of the sandbag wall, looking straight up in the sky full of stars. There was no air pollution in Vietnam, so the sky was clear and the millions of stars were big and bright. It was beautiful. Looking at the broad expanse of stars, a bright white light that was bigger and brighter than any star came into view floating across the sky. I watched it for a while expecting to hear the sound of a plane. But there was no sound and the night was dead quiet. The light would move fast in a straight line, then stop suddenly, unlike an airplane. It started up again in a different direction then stopped again, always moving in a straight line. It did this back and forth across the sky for several minutes. There was still no sound. Airplanes don't fly like this. I poked my buddy and said, "See that light. What is it?" Maybe I was just seeing things. He looked, saw the light, and watched for a while. We couldn't determine what it was. A few minutes later it appeared to move directly away from us, becoming smaller and smaller, then finally disappearing. It was a UFO, of course, since we couldn't identify it.

We had no action that night on guard duty. Other nights some guards caught bad guys trying to get on the airfield, but for the most part it was quiet at night. A couple of times Vietnamese girls tried to sneak onto base at night to visit some guys. Some of our guys would also try to sneak off base at night. Risky business either direction, for a lot of reasons.

One time our whole company, about a hundred and eighty people, became very ill with hot and cold flashes, fever, weakness and diarrhea, in varying degrees of severity. Our company medical people, while treating everyone the best they could, got on the problem right away and tried to identify the illness as well as the cause. Malaria was a real risk but we all took malaria pills daily so that was not likely the problem. Another possibility was dysentery that one could easily get from bad water or contaminated food. Our officers' club was first to be checked, but we only served officers, no enlisted guys, and everyone was sick. It was found to be clean. After a day or two, the medical staff found that the illness was coming from our mess hall where everyone ate. It was dysentery. We had Vietnamese women and girls working in the kitchen as well as cleaning. They apparently hadn't been washing properly before preparing and handling food. *Probably after using our shitters. Nice thought.*

It was also very possible that someone was intentionally sabotaging the unit. We knew that we had Vietcong among the people who came in to work on our base during the day and making all of us sick would be an effective strike against our mission effectiveness. We kept our eyes open all the time for suspicious activity on base since the bad guys would try to hurt us anyway they could. The Vietnamese people around us were never completely trusted. A certain amount of exposure always existed. I usually carried my loaded personal side arm with me everywhere I went.

The dysentery was bad news. We had some guys so sick that it was all they could do to get up and walk to the shitter and back to bed. They were very weak, couldn't eat and keep anything down. We assigned some guys who were less sick to stay with some of the sicker guys around the clock. Meanwhile flying our missions had to continue. Some guys would just shit in their flight suits while flying and clean up when they got back to base. A crew chief would sometimes have to wash out the helicopter with buckets of water. I did the flight scheduling for our gun platoon at this time, along with being the club officer. My dysentery wasn't too bad, but I had work to do on the ground, so flew only a few days during this time. It took a couple of weeks for everyone to get back to normal. There was no Imodium AD. It was not a fun time.

One time our mission took us up north and east of base to provide gun cover for an Agent Orange defoliation spray operation. It was an all day mission flying cover for a single Huey spray ship, set up with the usual twenty foot long spray pipes extending out each side of the helicopter. Barrels of Agent Orange were loaded on board then the orange goo was pumped out the pipe booms and out several spray nozzles into the air as the aircraft was flown slowly right on the tree tops. This was supposedly going to be a rather peaceful day. The ground commander in the area, a Vietnamese officer, told us that all of the territory we were to fly over had been secured by his troops, so it was completely safe. We were instructed not to do any firing of any kind, no matter what occurred. That sounded good.

We flew out to the area and made one long pass, flying behind the spray ship providing cover, then went back for another load of Agent Orange. Since we could not do any shooting, our plan was to simply provide the best cover possible by flying slowly and at a perfect target altitude. A second gunship was flying with me as my wingman. We made ourselves a nice juicy target, a better target than the spray ship that flew right on the trees ahead of us, in an attempt to draw enemy fire to us if there was going to be any.

About half way through our second pass life suddenly became very exciting. Two or three enemy with AK 47's opened up on us. Our orders were to not fire under any circumstances, so we could not shoot, even to protect ourselves. We immediately started taking multiple bullet hits in the helicopter. As bullets were ripping through our airframe, I quickly dove to my left into an opening in the jungle. Flying low over the ground behind trees, we were able to screen ourselves partially from the enemy fire. The spray ship had quickly departed up ahead of us.

We got some distance away and the firing stopped. We were fortunate that none of us on board was hit. A lot of heavy, accurate fire had hit our helicopter. I checked all my instruments and everything looked okay for the moment, so we headed back to the stage field where our spray operation was based.

Once on the ground we inspected our gunship. We found major bullet damage through the belly and into the interior airframe structure, as well as many holes in our rotor blades, and some in the inner blade reinforced laminate area that leads to the blade grips. We also found one hole all the way through our tail boom about an inch below our tail rotor driveshaft that was big enough to stick your arm through. We could see daylight all the way through our tail where several bullets had impacted. Flying as slowly as we had been, we would have begun spinning like a top if our tail rotor driveshaft had been severed. This would not have been a good way to make contact with the ground. Two bullets had also impacted our bomb rack on the right side, heading directly at our gunner, but had been deflected. A couple of inches higher and he would have been hit. It was another close call. Due to the major damage to our helicopter, a Chinook heavy lift company was called to come hook on to it and drag it home on a strap, again. We rode back to base in the Chinook, above our disabled gunship.

I didn't talk further with the Vietnamese commander. It seems he was nowhere around. He may have been out trying to find the VC who were apparently part of his unit, or maybe he was hiding from me. I still carried my loaded side arm. Next time he could go flying with me.

I later found out that I had been awarded the Vietnamese Cross of Gallantry by the Vietnamese government for the action, and we never fired a shot. The bad guys almost got some kills, however. I would be awarded several other awards before the year was out, including thirty seven Air Medals, a few with V device for valor, and a Bronze Star for meritorious achievement against hostile forces.

About this time we were due for a unit CMMI Inspection. This was our one big command readiness inspection during the year. It was the Command Manpower & Material Inventory inspection.

Virtually all areas of our unit operation were going to be inspected by the Inspector General's office, from front office operations, to flight, aircraft maintenance, to weapons operations. This was an important inspection and our whole unit stood down for several days with everyone working to prepare for the big day.

Every unit has what is called a TO&E, table of organization and equipment, which is a complete list of all the personnel and equipment a unit was supposed to have in order to fulfill its mission. In preparation, inventories were taken in all areas and stock was organized and arranged for physical inspection. Inspections are a big thing in the military.

In our aircraft maintenance and weapons maintenance areas we often held on to good parts that were useful for backing up day to day operations. You never knew when extra helicopter or engine parts, or weapons parts, would be needed. We were breaking helicopters and burning out machine gun barrels daily. Our maintenance people were busy overnight every night fixing helicopters that were shot up or broken, making them ready for combat operations the next morning. As a result of this ongoing activity and getting regular new supply shipments from stateside, we ended up with a lot of extra parts. Many parts were serviceable and we had an overstock of many items. However, we were not supposed to have more of any of the items listed on our TO&E, and certainly not less.

A few days before the CMMI inspection, I flew a mission that was more than a little out of the ordinary. A helicopter was loaded with perfectly good extra parts, like rocket launcher tubes, machine gun barrels, whole machine guns, aircraft parts, and many other items. We then flew out over the Mekong River, downriver to an area away from civilization, and dumped everything overboard. *What a waste. Tax dollars at work!* Our inspection went well, though, and our commander probably got a medal.

Speaking of tax dollars at work, we often flew with two 19-shot rocket pods, one mounted on each side of the gunship, for a total of 38 rockets. I could launch all 38 rockets in about 12 seconds. The cost for a load of rockets was around six thousand dollars. We seldom launched all our rockets in 12 seconds, but we quite regularly launched them all within a few minutes. We then would fly to rearming somewhere, reload, and launch another full compliment of rockets. We commonly did this four to six times a day, sometimes more. We had real firepower if we needed to use it. It was a real kick but it was expensive.

We fired the 2.75 inch diameter folding fin aerial rocket from our gunships. The rockets were five to six feet long depending on the size of warhead attached to the front of the rocket. This was the standard rocket that the Air Force used on many of its fighters. There were a couple different kinds of warheads and different fuses used that screwed on to the nose of the rocket. One was the typical high explosive warhead that we normally used, and another was a special fleschette warhead that contained four thousand brass darts. The fleschette rocket was used on specific missions against enemy troops. The darts were about an inch long and tightly packed in the warhead. When the rocket warhead exploded after launching, the darts were dispersed much like a shotgun would disperse shot. The sharp brass darts would cover a wide area on the ground and penetrate just about anything. It was a devastating personnel weapon.

Warhead fuses screwed onto the nose of the rocket warhead. The basic type of fuse we used simply caused the warhead to blow up on impact with anything, such as a bunker, a sampan, a hooch, a tree, the ground, etc. We hit a lot of trees when we fired into the jungle. The explosion would quite often cut the tree off, which would shake and fall over. It was interesting to see, but meaningless. We also used what was called a VT fuse. VT was short for *variable time*. This fuse contained a small radar unit in the nose. When a rocket was fired, the small radar unit on the nose would turn on arming the warhead. When the rocket traveled toward a target and got to within three feet of anything, a tree, a bunker, an enemy trooper, etc., the warhead would explode. These VT fused warheads fired into the jungle would often blow up in the trees, effectively being an air burst that sprayed the ground with shrapnel. It was very effective against any enemy combatants who were unfortunate enough to be in the vicinity.

One afternoon, I was flying very low over rice paddies doing reconnaissance in an area that was a free fire zone. There was a beautiful picturesque grass hut about a hundred yards away on the edge of the jungle. It was a pretty scene with green palm trees around the tan colored grass hut. No people were noticed around the area. I fired a rocket and it went directly into the side of the hut. The hut immediately blew up in a flaming mushroom cloud of red and yellow flame and burning grass. The explosion rose into the air with the classic mushroom shape we've often seen, quickly rising to some two hundred feet. It was quite a sight. It apparently had been a fuel storage hut. There might well have been VC inside. *The enemy would at least have to adjust their gas inventory.*

One night, our mission was to fly over west near the Cambodian border in an area called the Tram. The Tram was a large flooded area near the Mekong River that had once been heavily treed. The trees were dead and dry now, and there was a lot of wood cutting there during the day. At night, this area was also a place of regular infiltration of troops, weapons, and munitions into South Vietnam, by the NVA, from the Ho Chi Minh Trail. We were going to put in rocket strikes in the area, all night long. We would be using fleschette rockets, the one with the darts. We would start our work around eleven o'clock at night and quit as it started getting light the following morning.

Since it was dark, we couldn't see anything on the ground and could not identify any targets. There was a mobile radar site nearby at our refueling and rearming point, as well as a field artillery unit. There was a low hanging cloud layer that we flew in and out of while watching our flight instruments. It was interesting flying. We flew all night long on radar control. Our routes of flight and our altitudes were given to us by the radar controllers who were talking to us constantly. We usually flew at one thousand feet of altitude on a heading given us by the controllers, and then on their command we would start firing our flechette rockets remaining in level flight. We fired a pair of rockets every five seconds or so.

After we had expended all our rockets and had pretty well nailed the area down with darts, the artillery gun would fire parachute flares high overhead lighting up the area into which we had just fired. We had to be careful not to fly into the descending flares. Under the bright light from the flares we dropped down low and looked for ripples in the water. The door gunners would open up with their machineguns on any areas where they saw ripples, and my copilot shot his 40 millimeter cannon. We never saw what was in the water, but something there was still alive and moving. *We probably killed some otters. Maybe more.* We followed this routine all night refueling and rearming as necessary, then headed back to base at daybreak. It was an interesting night and the flying was fun.

One afternoon, on a day when I was not scheduled to fly, our maintenance officer asked me to fly over to Vung Tau with him to pick up some aircraft parts. It sounded like it would be a nice flight and a chance to see Vung Tau again, so we headed out about two o'clock, 1400 hours, and flew east in a D model Huey, one of our newer helicopters. The flight over was a nice afternoon flight with the sun in the sky behind us. We were flying by ourselves, single ship. Our route of flight took us over some old villages along some of the river tributaries that were interesting to see from the air but not altogether friendly territory on the ground. VC were known to be all over the area. We climbed up to a safe altitude of around five thousand feet for the flight over.

The flight over to Vung Tau was uneventful and we landed at the same airfield where I had attended Cobra School. As we were hovering to a parking place about three feet above the ground, as directed by the control tower, our engine quit. We did a hovering autorotation that we had practiced many times during flight school and gently sat the helicopter on the ground. We rolled our throttle off to flight idle, preparing to turn our fuel switch off and shut down the engine but noticed that the engine was still running at idle. When we brought the engine back up to operating rpm and did some checks, everything looked normal. We lifted up, continued to hover to our parking place and just as we arrived the engine quit again, so we executed another hovering autorotation at our parking place. Shutting things down, we went to the local maintenance shop to report the problem before heading across the airfield to get our parts.

After getting our parts we went back to the maintenance shop to check on our aircraft. The maintenance guys said they could not find anything wrong, but had drained some fuel from the various strainers and drains. It might have just been some contaminated fuel with dirt or water in it. It was getting late and we wanted to get back to Dong Tam, so we decided to crank up, do some good run-up checks, and see how things looked. I was with our maintenance officer so he was the expert. *Right!* We did various engine power checks at hover and everything looked fine, so we called the tower for clearance to depart and took off headed toward home.

By now it was nearly dark and we were headed west over some very unfriendly territory toward home base, alone. No gun cover this time. The engine seemed to be running fine and we made the hour plus flight home without any problems. As we were landing back at Dong Tam, stopping low above the ground at a hover, our engine quit again. *What was going on?* After another hovering autorotation we settled to the ground. The engine was still running at idle. We picked up again to hover to our own unit across the airfield and park in one of our parking places. By now, the engine had decided to not run well at all. The helicopter could not even make it the hundred yards to our unit, so we shut everything down and left it parked where we were and walked back to our unit with the new parts.

Looking back, I wonder what on earth we were thinking, taking off into night time over enemy territory, with a helicopter that had just previously not been running right. *Write this one off to another bit of good luck.* We felt pretty good that we'd made it back without having an engine failure along the way. That would not have been a pleasant experience. There had been stories of guys who went down in the very area we flew over and were never heard from again. *But again, all's well that ends well. Back to work the next day.*

CHAPTER 9

MOVING ON

June had arrived and, having been in this "sunny vacation land" for some time, my year was wearing on. I was sending letters home to my wife about twice a week or so, and to my folks a couple of times a month. Letters came back to me at about the same frequency. A few letters were also sent to my brother, Paul, who was stationed in Alaska in the Air Force. Letters from home were the only link any of us had with friends and family, and with what we considered normal life back stateside. There was no telephone service to home, certainly no email or satellite phones like today.

We did have armed forces television out of Saigon, with regular news programs, that also kept us informed about what was going on back in the States. We saw and heard all about the demonstrations against the war that were taking place. Those demonstrations generally pissed off all military guys in Vietnam, most being draftees, who had answered their call to duty and were putting their lives on the line every day. We were all disappointed that we didn't have more moral support from fellow Americans, as we were supporting our country's priorities and decisions, right or wrong. Vietnam veterans still are not "fonda Jane", if you remember her visit to North Vietnam. That was more than a slap in the face. It was treasonous in our opinion.

There were some guys, mostly among the enlisted ranks in Vietnam, who openly opposed the war, seemingly siding with the demonstrators back home. We all knew that the war was political by its very nature and screwed up in many ways. Most individuals performed their responsibilities the best they could, while others fought back as they could while performing their duties in minimal fashion. In my opinion, officers uniformly performed responsibly, following the Officers' Creed of *Duty, Honor, Country.*

The understood peace sign at the time was a hand in the air with the first two fingers extended straight up making a V-shaped symbol. It's still an understood peace sign today. A hand wave with the V peace symbol was a common salutation between military guys. It was effectively saying, *Hi, brother, peace.* I used the V sign a few times to be one of the guys. It was considered a minor and acceptable form of protest. After what we were seeing and doing it was sort of acknowledging that there might be better alternatives than war. Peace is not a bad thing after all. The saying, *Make love, not war,* also became popular during this era. Love is always a better choice than war. Maybe hippies and other peaceniks had it right.

Some protests took a more serious form. A couple of times we had reports that American soldiers had been spotted actively working with the Viet Cong in our area. They had defected to the enemy and were engaging in military operations with the VC, against the American military. They always had to keep their heads down, well hidden, and stay out of sight of any American military units. They were especially valuable targets. Some Special Forces and Navy Seals teams occasionally went out and tried to get them, but never have much luck.

There was some suspected sabotage specific to our unit, as well. One morning we were taking off from Ben Tre, the stage field south of our base, and were climbing up to altitude. As we got up to about one thousand feet and were turning left, heading out to the AO (area of operation), there was a loud *BOOM* back in the engine. We immediately experienced a significant loss of power and our EGT indication started to fluctuate. We descended back into Ben Tre and landed with partial power. Upon inspecting our engine, we saw that the first couple stages of our compressor vanes in the front of the jet engine were severely damaged, with some vanes broken off completely.

Later, when our maintenance people inspected the engine, they found parts of a metal fastener that was used to hold cowling on the helicopter. We had no fasteners missing. It appeared that someone, probably a mechanic or helper, had dropped a fastener into the inlet of our engine so the engine would ingest the metal and would fail at some point early in the day. The engine was trashed. There was an investigation, but no one was ever identified as a saboteur. We all kept an eye open for anyone involved in misdeeds around our area, friend or foe.

On another fairly routine day, my gunship fire team flew gun cover for some ground troops over to the west. My usual wingman was flying behind, covering my actions. We were working an area near a small village with a canal running through it. As we flew into the area I noticed several guys in dirty white pajamas moving quickly away from some bunkers, herding a few water buffalo across an open rice paddy. This was very suspicious because they were moving as quickly as they could. *Why did they need to move the water buffalo so fast? Answer, they were bad guys and were trying to get away.* The VC often would pretend to be local people working in the fields or herding animals. They sure looked like VC to me, and by now I'd had some good experience identifying Viet Cong. I called our C&C high overhead and asked for permission to fire on them. Word came back, a little slow, that the local province chief on board said no, we could not fire on them.

A few seconds later C &C called back and told me about a sampan motoring down the canal away from the action. Permission was given to fire and kill the single occupant. I flew over and took a look. The sampan was motoring slowly down the middle of the canal with an old, gray haired Vietnamese guy in it. I circled around and looked in the boat and at the old guy. There were no bundles, weapons, or anything suspicious and the old guy looked innocent enough to me. So I didn't fire on him, but rather turned away and continued on with the mission in another area.

It was stupid that we were given permission to take out an old Vietnamese man while the VC were allowed to walk away. The situation was disgusting. I could have been wrong of course, but doubt it. Interestingly, people could live or die every day from simple choices we made, right or wrong. We gunship pilots were not just mindless killers as this book and our general reputation may suggest. Often we would decide not to shoot for a variety of reasons.

One evening a story was told about a couple of our gunships that were working an area earlier that day, supporting ground troops in typical fashion. They were working down low with the ground troops and were flying around a hooch that was burning. The area of dry rice paddy around the hooch was also on fire. One of the crewmen in the back of one gunship noticed a naked baby sitting on some bare ground near the burning hooch crying. There were no adults around. The pilot landed away from the fire, the crewman jumped out and ran through the fire, picked up the baby and ran back to the helicopter. They flew the baby to a nearby village and handed it off to a mama-san, then rejoined the action. We often had a larger view of life than what was going on around us in combat operations. Innocent human life should always trump simple body count. We had some humanity in spite of everything.

About now our unit was ordered to move from Dong Tam to Can Tho which was about two hundred miles to the southwest. We didn't fly as much while preparing for the move. All units at Dong Tam were moving to other locations and the whole base was being left to the Vietnamese military. It was one way we were supporting the build up of Vietnamese forces.

We pretty much stripped our facilities at Dong Tam of anything we thought might be useful at our next base. In general, we weren't particularly fond of the Vietnamese military and didn't feel that we needed to leave them much of anything. We took all plumbing, sinks, and faucets from the shower room, all electrical wires and outlets, all wall paneling, door hinges, etc. In other words, we stripped the place. We took everything out of our officers' club/bunker. We had some old booze left over and some of the guys who were particularly "fond" of the Vietnamese opened the bottles and splashed the booze all over the walls, floor and ceiling. They really washed the place down. It was so rank inside that one had to hold his breath when going in to check it out. It was basically uninhabitable. *Welcome Mister Vietnamese Soldier, part time Viet Cong. I hope nobody struck a match in there.*

While doing a little research on line, I found that Dong Tam today is the site of a venomous snake farm. They supposedly raise poisonous snakes there and milk them for the venom that is then used for snake bite treatment all over the world. *Interesting, and how fitting. We Copperheads were snakes as well.*

Primary Helicopter Flight School Honor Graduate.
I graduated number 1 in my flight class of 140 students.

My flight school class 68-36-B2

A typical road on base

View of part of our company area. Airfield is at top where we parked our helicopters. Our Operations shack is on the left and aircraft maintenance on the right.

More company area at Dong Tam. Shitter is on the left and bunker / officers' club on the right. Our BOQ, officer's quarters, is directly behind me when taking this picture.

Our bunker / officers, club behind the bar. Dick, my roommate, and Tue, our bar maid. Notice the heavy wood beams.

Outside the door to my room in our BOQ at Dong Tam.

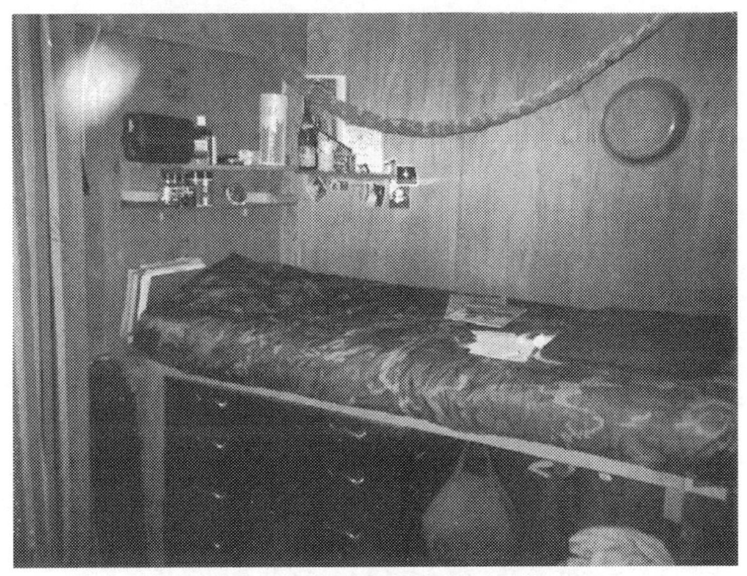

My bed on a wooden frame over my dresser with a small bunker behind.

The northern branch of the Mekong River. Dong Tam was off the picture to the left across the river.

C Model Huey gunship parked in a protective L shaped revetment on the airfield. Rocket pod is visible on the left side and 40 millimeter cannon on the nose.

Main road from Dong Tam to My Tho, a small Vietnamese village two miles east. I was out driving around seeing the sights with another guy on a day when we were not flying.

The AH1G Cobra. The Cobra had a maximum airspeed of about 240 miles per hour.

The Cobra was narrow, fast and could be unforgiving if not flown correctly.

The cockpit in the Cobra. The flight and weapons systems were complex. It had a computer assisted flight control system.

My usual position in a C Model Huey gunship. I'm wearing the 30 lb. "Chicken Plate" body armor on my chest.

Me flying

A nineteen shot rocket pod mounted on the bomb rack. The Crew Chief is servicing the jet engine.

Part of the rearming location at Dong Tam. Notice the 2.75 inch diameter folding fin aerial rockets standing up against the storage box.

I was flying cover on the day when this lift ship was blown up in an LZ, killing an American Lieutenant.

Our Copperhead gun pilot patch that we wore on our flight suits.

Hooches of our gun platoon at Can Tho. The guy sitting in the chair was wounded one day in both legs and was air lifted out from the boonies. We never saw him again. We boxed his personal items and sent them home.

Outside my hooch at Can Tho. This was common attire on down days around our hooch during the hot season.

My hooch during morning coffee over a Sterno stove on the floor, with some of my guys. This is where we all enjoyed the box of cookie crumbs from home.

Our hooch maid. A nice gal.
She didn't understand a lick of English.

Some guys enjoying a down day during the hot, sunny dry season. Love that hot sunny weather!

Conditions during the wet monsoon season looking out my hooch. We never had dry boots.

Vietnamese women doing our laundry between our hooches. Our water was hauled daily in water trailers. Water was pumped from the Mekong River then purified.

Cajun on the right in front of a C Model gunship. The 40 millimeter cannon is on the nose. The guy on the left was flying copilot the day my friend Frank was killed.

Cajun was flying as my wingman one day and crashed 222, triple duce, after taking off behind me. Thankfully all the crew walked away without being seriously hurt.

The wide expanse of rice paddies between Can Tho and the mountains to the west. Notice another helicopter near center way off in the distance.

Mountains over west of Can Tho near the Cambodian border. I flew in these mountains a lot supporting Special Forces units.

My gunship being carried back to Can Tho by a Chinook heavy lift helicopter. The gunship is carried by a long strap under the Chinook.

These are ARVN, Army Republic of Vietnam Nam soldiers, our allies, that we worked with often.

This Snoopy cartoon was drawn for me by one of my gunship pilots. He crashed a few months later and died. I have it framed and hanging in my home.

Some of my awards. Top left is the Vietnamese Cross of Gallantry. An uncommon award given by the Vietnamese Government. The middle is the Air Medal. I earned 37 of these. On the right is the Bronze Star. The two bottom awards are basic awards for serving in Vietnam.

A brightly colored, hand painted Bengal tiger on thin silk purchased while down between missions near the village of Tan An north of Dong Tam. I have it framed and hanging in our home.

CHAPTER 10

CAN THO AND MORE ACTION

An advance party went to Can Tho a couple of months ahead of our move, to set up camp. Our unit would be living in tents and Southeast Asian huts, that we gun pilots were to occupy. On the night before our actual move down to Can Tho we had to sleep overnight anywhere we could, since our facilities had all been gutted. I chose to sleep in what used to be my hooch on the cement floor next to a large pile of trash. The interior of the building was open with all the paneling gone and no door. It was the first obvious choice to bed down and there was no better place apparent at the time. Crawling into my sleeping bag on the cement floor and trying to get comfortable, some light sleep did come. I was abruptly awakened in the middle of the night by an animal walking across my chest. When I realized that something was on me, I jumped and the animal ran away. It had to have been a rat. Rats were common all over Vietnam, some getting as big as house cats. The Vietnamese used to hunt them at night. They ate them. Red meat was premium fare.

The next morning we loaded up our helicopters for the flight to Can Tho, about an hour and a half away, and took off. We said *good-bye* to Dong Tam. We were happy to be leaving. It was indeed a hellhole, but still not as bad as some places. Our whole unit flew down to Can Tho in one large gaggle. There were about twenty helicopters. It was an interesting sight.

Our unit area at Can Tho was on the northwest corner of the air base and was bordered with barbed wire, guard towers and machine gun bunkers. We were located right on a portion of the base perimeter. Our whole area had been a swamp that was filled in with dirt. There was still swamp on the other side of our perimeter to the northwest. The gunship pilots were supposedly the elite pilots in our unit, so we lived in wood huts with clapboard siding and tin roofs, known as Southeast Asian huts, instead of tents. The upper two feet of the walls were screened up to the roofline for ventilation. It also let dust in. There was a dirt road on the south side of our company area that large trucks traveled on to a motor pool and my hooch was right next to the road. It was a very dusty, dirty place. I crawled in the sack every night with grit between my teeth. It was dusty in the dry season and our whole unit flooded during the rainy season. We never had dry feet during the rainy season.

The now famous Tet of '68, with all the coordinated attacks against U.S. forces around South Vietnam, occurred the year before I got there. Can Tho had been attacked at that time with some American soldiers killed and helicopters blown up. The NVA and VC captured and occupied about half the base and the American military had to fight most of a day and night to win it back.

One night a few months before we moved to Can Tho, the VC attacked the south perimeter of the base. They likely had been watching closely for some time and eventually found a bunker where all the guards were sleeping. The VC snuck in and killed all the guards by slitting their throats. They then went farther into the area where helicopters were parked, dropped explosive charges, and blew some up. There was constant exposure to the enemy along the perimeter but it was usually quiet. We constantly had to stay on guard. It was our responsibility, as a unit, to guard our area of the base perimeter at all times. A couple of times I was assigned duty as Officer of the Guard, covering a twenty-four hour period. Overnight was the worst. It was hard staying awake and keeping all the guards awake. But it was important to keep our unit and the airfield protected.

My extra duty assignment at Dong Tam had been Officer Club Officer. There was a large established officers' club on base at Can Tho, so we didn't have our own club in our unit. The extra duty of Awards and Decorations Officer was assigned to me for our unit. The responsibility in that position was to recommend members of our unit for certain awards and medals for combat related actions. Actions worthy of awards had to be identified, the details researched, and awards recommendations drafted and written up following standard military procedure. The recommendation package was then sent up the chain of command to Battalion which was an intermediate stop for further endorsements. It was then sent further up the chain in the awards process until the award was issued. Certain awards and medals were automatic for just being in Vietnam and other awards were for special actions. Awards were a big deal. Officers needed certain awards over time to advance higher and higher in rank. I thought one time (becoming a cynic by then) about applying for an award for myself for being the Awards and Decorations officer. Why not? Our infamous politicians in Washington vote for excess benefits for themselves all the time. But, unlike our politicians, I wouldn't stoop that low.

Along with Awards and Decorations Officer, I also assigned our gun pilots to daily flight duty, simply rotating my guys through a flight duty roster so the guys flew two, three or four days on, then had a couple of days off. Sometimes guys would request certain types of missions that they wanted to fly or other pilots they wanted to fly with. Guys were not scheduled to fly if they were sick or had something else they wanted to do. We were pretty flexible. All in all it worked out well.

The weather had been nice during this dry season. It was usually sunny and hot during the day then it would cool off at night, as soon as the sun went down. The temperature during midday often rose to over one hundred degrees and at night it routinely dropped down into the sixties. It was a little cloudy sometimes and there might be the occasional rain shower. I slept every night with an Army issued wool blanket over me, under my mosquito netting.

The dry season could be very hot at times. When we flew, we were required to wear our Nomex flight suits that were made of a thick wool-like material. The Nomex material was fire retardant and offered some protection if we ended up in a fire for some reason. We joked about it actually. We may not initially get burns on our body but we might end up baking to death.

Flight suits were especially uncomfortable when the weather was hot. It was required that we have our sleeves rolled all the way down and closed around our wrists. We also had to wear flight gloves that were made of Nomex with calfskin palms. Our Nomex flight suit legs were tucked in the top of our all leather boots or bloused at the top of our boots. We usually had our collars fastened tight around our neck to keep empty hot brass cartridges from going down our shirts when our machine gunners in the back were shooting. We were covered from head to toe in this fire retardant Nomex material with leather boots, gloves and helmet. Even with all this protection pilots and crew were still burned horribly in crashes. We also had our pistol and survival knife strapped on and wore a 30-pound chicken plate on our chest that was contained in a vest strapped around us. We were suited up for action but it could be hot.

When we were flying there was normally a breeze blowing through the helicopter that helped us stay a little cooler. When it was especially hot, flying to or from a mission briefing or back home at the end of the day, I would sometimes climb up to five to six thousand feet. It was cool up there and it was great relief from the heat. When we were shut down on the ground we would often take off our flight suit shirts and seek shade wherever we could find it. Sometimes the only shade was under our helicopter. Our helicopter would often be so hot sitting in the sun that you could not keep your hand on the outside metal surface more than a few seconds. It might have fried an egg. The helicopter always seemed to operate just fine no matter how hot the weather.

The rainy, monsoon season eventually arrived. During the monsoon season it was cloudy most of the time with low hanging clouds and it rained much of the time, almost every day. It was cool all the time and got colder at night. The cooler weather felt good. We kept flying our normal types of missions but the level of activity overall seemed to slow down some in the wet, cloudy, rainy conditions. The ground was much wetter and muddy. We kept up our same flying routines. We flew in the rain a lot. Sometimes the rain was so heavy that I had to open my window and stick my head out to keep sight of the ground. The windshield could be totally obscured. We often had trouble getting high enough to put in good rocket attacks. We just stayed low, sometimes between clouds, and fired the rockets from lower angles.

We still flew cover for our lift ships much of the time. We'd fly cover behind them when we were flying to and from an area of operation. Occasionally they would fly up into the clouds maintaining their formation flight into IFR conditions. They flew close formation so they were close enough to keep sight of each other even in the clouds. They would usually turn on their red rotating beacons to keep better sight of each other. We would loose sight of them from our gunships, being a distance behind and below them. These guys were good. We would stay down below the clouds in our gunships on the treetops if necessary and meet back up with the formation flight when they came out of the clouds. They had good cover hidden in the clouds. We were never taught this sort of flying in flight school. We learned a lot more about flying from actual demands in this combat environment. It was often interesting and challenging flying.

The mountains over on the Cambodian border was a great area to fly. It was beautiful, majestic, country with large flat areas of rice paddies around and mountains rising up some three or four thousand feet. There was an interesting, and classic military mentality in the mountains. Our ground troops occupied the peaks and ridgelines with small military outposts scattered along in strategic locations. Since we occupied the high ground we supposedly owned the mountains. The sides and the interior of the mountains were occupied by the Viet Cong and North Vietnamese Army, however. The mountains in this area were all honeycombed inside. They were full of tunnels and caves. At this one particular mountain, there was a road at ground level that led from the west into the mountain that was big enough to drive in a large truck. A couple of times, when having some time to kill, I flew low over the road heading into the mountain and fired several rockets into the opening trying to get my rockets as far inside as possible. Charlie may have only been awakened from a nice nap. They harassed us and we harassed them. And we killed each other when we could.

Our outposts on the peaks and ridgelines were supplied by helicopter. It was the only way to get there. There were no roads. We provided gun cover many times to resupply flights to the tops of mountains. The enemy occupied the mountains inside and down the sides, but we occupied the tops. The top was supposed to offer some military advantage. It didn't mean anything though. Being close to the Cambodian border, the mountains were valuable to the NVA and VC. They had supply storage and whole villages inside the mountains. Our guys on top were sometimes attacked at night, mostly unsuccessfully, and could never venture away from their secure outposts or they would be wiped out. Our guys had a good view though. Prime real estate. There are probably resorts up there now. It would be fun to go back and see the area today.

We flew operations in and around the mountains regularly. There was a deep rocky gulch in one area between two mountains cutting across open rice paddy. It was like a tunnel without the top. The gulch was being used routinely by the NVA to move people and material from one mountain to the other. We were called in one day to work in a combined operation with the Air Force, an Army infantry unit, a Vietnamese artillery unit, and an Army armor unit. The artillery unit would be shelling the side of the mountain to the west, and the Air Force hitting the mountain on the east with jet fighters dropping napalm, while the infantry unit moved up from the south on foot, and the armor unit moved down from the north in armored personnel carriers. They were boxing in the area and all moving toward the gulch.

As the mission got underway, we flew in over the deep gulch and attacked. The goal was to wipe out a large NVA unit that was reportedly moving between the two mountains. We apparently caught the NVA with their pants down. We fired rockets, mini-guns, machine guns, and 40 mm cannon into the gulch, where the bullets and shrapnel bounced all over in the rocky gulch. We killed and wounded many of the enemy. When the infantry finally arrived at the gulch and began mopping up, they reported a solid trail of blood and materials in the gulch going back up into the mountains but not many bodies. The bad guys who were able took most of their dead and wounded with them and moved back up into the mountains.

It was not a good day for Mister Charles. It was an exciting operation with all the exploding artillery and napalm erupting into flames all around us. I'll never forget the setting, the sights and the action on that day.

CHAPTER 11

REST AND RELAXATION

It was now August, and my wife and I had been apart for eight months. We were ready to spend some time together on R&R (rest and relaxation). My requested time off was approved and we made plans to meet in Honolulu, Hawaii. It took some time to put a plan together considering that a letter home took two weeks and a return letter another two weeks. I let my wife know my scheduled arrival time, then relied on her to reserve a hotel room and travel to Hawaii by herself from the States. She got other necessary information from the military and planned the flight to Honolulu. A military wife's airfare on a regular commercial airlines was especially cheap. Our plan was to meet at the reception area at the small Army base right on Waikiki beach in Honolulu, late in the afternoon on a certain day in August. We each had to do our own thing and hope it worked out.

It was a pleasant surprise when our plan came together. After flying to Saigon on a helicopter courier flight from my base in the boonies, staying overnight in a block building on a cot, catching a ride the next day to a busy congested military flight terminal at the airport and hopping on a plane, I amazingly arrived some time later at the airport in Honolulu. A military bus then transferred the plane load of us to town. We made our way off the bus at the reception center and as I walked through the door into the lobby, there was my wife waiting for me. What a wonderful sight after eight months. It was, and still is, sort of a blur. Modern day travel coordination didn't exist, but we had managed to come together from opposite sides of the world at the planned time.

For wives or girlfriends who were looking forward to meeting their guys in Hawaii, or at other places around the world, it would sometimes be a huge disappointment. Plans didn't always work out. My wife mentioned from information she received before leaving the states, and from a briefing she received in Hawaii, that sometimes the guys they were waiting for wouldn't show up. And it was impossible to know why at that point. There were a few women in my wife's group that day whose guys didn't show up. As part of the greeting of our large group at the reception center, we all noticed that some of the wives or girlfriends standing there waiting did not greet anyone getting off our bus. It was not a pleasant sight, but they were noticed only briefly. They were quickly taken aside to a private room by military people, separating them from the otherwise happy group. They were given information regarding what the options were.

The late soldiers would sometimes show up in the next day or two, so the women often waited. Some guys would never show up. It might have been simple coordination problems, but some women simply had to fly back home after a few days, still not knowing what the problem had been. It was nearly impossible to contact anyone directly to get information. This must have been a gut wrenching experience. There were some instances where guys were wounded or killed in action before they could made it to their planned R&R. That was not a good deal for anyone.

My one small checked bag actually arrived with me on the same airplane. We were supposed to wait at the reception center for the bag that was due shortly on a separate truck, but my wife grabbed me and we headed out on foot to the Princess Kilianni Hotel several blocks away, where she had rented a room for the next week. We were not concerned about my bag right then after being apart for eight months. We would get the bag later. There was not really much in it of value anyway, just some dirty military stuff and some toiletries. My wife had brought civilian clothes with her for me to wear. Olive drab green clothes were all I had, which was not a very pleasant Polynesian color, and they likely didn't smell very good.

We didn't sleep much that first night but we weren't watching TV! Well, maybe some. It was a nice reunion. We slept in the following morning and woke up to sweet smelling air, a warm breeze and bright sunshine in peaceful, quiet Hawaii. What a wonderful change from Vietnam. We went out the next day and started eating some good food at different restaurants. It was the first really good food I'd had in the last eight months. It seems like we spent a lot of time in restaurants during the next few days. We did get a lot of rest and ate lot of good food. Our hotel had a beautiful pool in a side courtyard with poolside snacks and a bar. We spent hours in the sun by the pool smelling the especially sweet smells of Hawaii. I still love Hawaii. My experience on R&R and the stark contrast with Vietnam is probably why.

One afternoon I got a Hawaiian punch drink from the bar, in a big bowl with an orchid floating on top. The bartender said it was a mix of five different rums and pineapple juice. Drinking it probably too fast, I promptly went to sleep in the sun on a lounge chair. I don't think I moved a muscle all afternoon. It was great. It was the best sleep I'd had in many months.

One evening we went to a nice Mexican restaurant on the main street along Waikiki, just a few blocks from our hotel, and got the biggest meal on the menu. I ordered a big plate of various Mexican foods plus chips, salsa, Mexican beer and dessert. We were stuffed after this great meal. We walked out of the restaurant and were standing on the sidewalk, breathing in and out deeply, when we noticed a German restaurant across the street. Some good German food sure sounded good. So we walked across the street and both ordered a full German meal. I had wiener schnitzel with sauerkraut and some good German beer. What a treat! Now we were very much over stuffed. We somehow made our way out of the restaurant and slowly walked back to our room. It took a day or so to recover from that experience. But it sure was a nice change from military food from a mess hall, in a tent, with a dirt floor, with a plastic fork, or eating C rations out in the boonies. Another evening, we went to a fancy French restaurant. It was too fancy for us but the food was good.

We spent a lot of time on the beach, in the water and in the sun. We also walked around town, went to the zoo, rented a car and toured the island. I loved the place. Hawaii was a wonderful place compared to where I had just come from. I would return several times in later years and still love it today.

The week went by too fast. It was soon going to be time for us to say goodbye again and return to our separate lives half a world apart. I don't remember many details of this time. Talk can be a little difficult in this sort of situation and we didn't talk a lot. Having experience with my "work" in Vietnam, I knew very well what the risks were, and that this could easily be our last goodbye, but we didn't talk about it. Not much information was offered to my wife regarding my work and flying in Vietnam when we were together. And she didn't ask any probing questions. We must have felt it was best left alone. Why ruin the wonderful Hawaii experience? There's not much one can say sometimes, beyond the obvious expressions of caring for each other.

We would say our goodbye at the reception center where we said our hello a short week before. I was transitioning back into my combat state of mind by now and likely was coming across distant and rather cool. This was a chilling experience. We didn't want to separate again. It was especially hard saying goodbye this time knowing what I was returning to. All you can do after the hugs and kisses is just turn and walk away.

I got back on the bus to the airport, crawled onto the airplane, then blasted off on the flight back to Saigon. My wife would stay for another day before flying back stateside to Kalamazoo. My working mindset quickly returned on the flight to Saigon. I got another courier flight down to Can Tho and checked back in with my unit. It was a nice R&R, in a beautiful place, with my lovely wife, but I was somehow content, maybe resigned, to be back with the guys at Can Tho, sort of writing off the very pleasant previous week. It was a strange feeling.

As a gunship pilot I could have taken three R&R's. Some of our pilots traveled to various places around the world together. Travel to Hawaii again, or to some other exotic place like Australia, Hong Kong, or Japan would have been great. Being so actively involved in military operations and busy flying, however, I didn't have much interest in taking any more time off. It seemed like too much trouble having to coordinate and plan travel out of Vietnam, even though other places sounded interesting. So I didn't go on any more R&R's. Time was passing quickly and I just wanted to complete my tour and return home. Looking back, the opportunity to travel to other places should not have been squandered.

CHAPTER 12

ANGEL ON MY SHOULDER

Time was continuing to move along a day at a time. This being August and having been in country for some time, I knew my way around pretty well. Routine had been pretty well established. They said in flight school training that the better you do your job, the better your chances of survival. This was no doubt true. By this time, I had already had many close calls and been able to walk away or fly my way out of trouble. Lady Luck had been on my side, although I was beginning to feel that luck alone was not the only force that influenced whether good or bad things happened. Luck alone was too simple a notion somehow. How could one be so lucky? Many times the feeling was that there must be a guardian angel around, maybe sitting on my shoulder. Maybe this angel was influencing the missions we flew.

One time we were working an area ahead of ground troops doing our usual snoop and poop and noticed a couple of people up ahead of us, a half mile away or so, run into a bunker. The bunker was alongside an open rice paddy. We flew ahead to pursue the suspected VC. We had permission to shoot up the area in preparation for the ground troops, so my wingman and I climbed to some altitude and set up for a rocket attack on the bunker. We started our rocket attack in usual fashion flying a left racetrack pattern. I made my first run on the bunker firing four or five rockets. None of my rockets came even close, which was a bit unusual. A bunker like this could usually be hit with at least one rocket from the total fired. I had become a pretty accurate shot with rockets. Climbing back to altitude after each attack, my wingman and I each made two more runs on the bunker in the next few minutes. None of our rockets impacted any closer than ten feet away or so. Not close enough to do any damage to the bunker. We were a bit frustrated with not hitting the target.

The ground troops were getting closer, so we stopped shooting. The troops surrounded the bunker and told the people to come out. As we flew overhead and watched, the door to the bunker opened and out walked a mama-san (a Vietnamese mother) and a young girl, eight or nine years old. They were probably mother and daughter. *Whew!*

I remember having a very strange feeling. A chill ran through me, although it was a hot day. It was a relief that we had missed our target with our rockets. I had a strong feeling that there had been some force around us that kept our rockets away from that bunker. It was as though the mother and daughter had been protected. Maybe it was my guardian angel, or maybe theirs. Maybe we shared the angel. The ground troops questioned the two people then let them go on their way. It was a very good day, this day with no kills. Sometimes good things happened in Vietnam.

Another time working an area west of Can Tho, supporting ground troops, flying our usual snoop and poop, shooting up the area, we were flying low level on the treetops when we saw some armed VC run into a hooch near a canal, in a grove of trees. After getting a little altitude in preparation for a rocket attack, and setting up a racetrack attack pattern, we were still pretty low. We started our rocket attack from about two thousand feet going into a fairly steep dive, but wouldn't be able to stay on target long because the ground would come up fast. My wingman and I made a run or two and completely missed the hooch.

On my last dive on target my rockets went long over the target. We were just too close. A bit upset with myself, I pushed the stick further forward into an even steeper dive to make one last try. Firing one last pair of rockets, I saw the ground coming up really fast and didn't watch to see if I had hit the target. Seeing that the helicopter had dropped way too low during the steep dive, I abruptly pulled the nose up and pulled full power with my collective control. The rotor speed began dropping below normal operating rpm with maximum power. It was going to be real close pulling out of my dive before hitting the ground. This was a common mistake made by gunship pilots flying low. The 540 rotor system on our C Model Huey, the same system used on the Cobra, will supply a maximum of 13,000 pounds of thrust, no more, simply due to its engineered design. Attempting to get more lift from the rotor system than the engine could power, my rotor speed was bleeding off, and the ground was coming up fast.

This was an *Oh Shit* moment for sure, which is not a good reaction when one is flying. With no time to think, my training took over. Under full power and sinking fast, I side slipped the helicopter to the left over a canal that happened to be nearby. It would be better I figured to hit water than hard ground. The water in the canal was also some ten feet or so below ground level so that would also give us a bit more effective altitude. Every foot would count. As we neared the water, I was able to bring the nose of the gunship up stopping our descent, barely keeping my skids out of the water. With our rotor speed still low, I yanked on the collective, jumped up over the edge of the canal onto a dry rice paddy, and came to a full stop on the ground.

We sat there for a few seconds while our rotor speed built back up into the green normal operating range then took off and climbed back up to altitude. There was no longer any interest in anyone who might still be in that hooch. *Funny thing.* Instead we flew on to other action on the mission around the area. Finishing the day in more normal fashion, we were able to fly back to base and have a beer at the officers' club. It was a tough life, my guardian angel had come through again.

On a similar day we were working low level around a hooch that some bad guys had run into. My door gunner had a shoulder fired M79 grenade launcher, which was like a large shotgun but fired a 40 millimeter, about two inch, high explosive projectile. I was maneuvering the gunship very low below the surrounding treetops to get my gunner close to the hooch. He was going to blow the roof off and maybe set the hooch on fire. As I was flying around the hooch, I was watching the green trees all around out of the corner of my eye. All of a sudden my crew chief yelled, "Look out!" Looking up quickly, I saw a completely dead tree that had been bleached almost white in the sun, right in front of the helicopter. And we were about to fly right into it. Immediately pulling collective pitch and pulling back on the stick, the helicopter came to a stop in front of the tree. We then climbed up and over it. We would have cut a bunch of firewood if we'd flown into the tree. It was a close call. *Thanks crew chief.* Everyone on board was all eyes and ears when we flew. It often took all of us watching out for trouble to be able to fly home in one piece at the end of a day. Going home to supper after a long day is a good thing.

Life on base at the airfield was okay in spite of living on a dusty road. One just had to accept the conditions. There was a PX (post exchange) on base that was sort of like a small variety store. It had a selection of items that troops in a combat zone might need or want such as toiletries, as well as many other things. There was even Tang to mix with our water from the Mekong River, so it was decent enough to drink. I bought a good Omega watch there that I still have. It quit running a long time ago though.

We also got our hair cut on base near our officers' club. It was a real treat. The barbershop was a small wooden shack with three Vietnamese barbers. They had regular barber chairs, compliments of American taxpayers I'm sure. We all kept our hair cut pretty short so there was never much styling involved. I got a kick out of the haircut routine. It was a pleasant experience every month or so. For $1.25 MPC (military pay certificate) which included a tip, you got a shampoo, blow dry, haircut, a scalp massage, as well as a facial, neck and shoulder massage. During the massage routine the barber would grab hold of your head with one hand on the back of your head and one hand on your chin and twist your head hard to the left, then hard to the right. You could feel and hear the sharp snap in the neck. It hurt for a split second but it left one really relaxed. It felt like your head could swivel all the way around. These guys really knew what they were doing. I've never had a haircut stateside that has even come close to what those guys could do.

From time to time, as the barber was shaving my hairline with a straight razor, I wondered if he might be a VC off base at night. A quick slip of that razor, intentional or otherwise, and one's life would end. Not a fitting end for a gunship pilot. Besides it would have messed up the barbershop and he would have lost his good paying job. So I figured I was safe enough. He would have chosen a higher ranking officer to slice up anyway.

On days that we flew, we would typically get up around 4:30 in the morning, get dressed, go to the mess hall for breakfast, to flight operations to receive our mission information for the day, then to the flight line and ready our gunships. We would often take off around sun up. The days could be long.

One day started out normally. It was a beautiful morning when we took off into the low hanging sunrise, turned left and headed up north to Vinh Long for a mission briefing with ground commanders who we were to work with for the day. It was about a twenty minute flight north of our base. We were fully loaded with fuel, rockets and other munitions that put us at or a bit above gross designed weight for the aircraft, almost 13,000 pounds. We were heavy. We had just turned north climbed to a few thousand feet when my emergency caution warning panel lit up, flashing red and orange, and the loud beeping emergency warning horn blasted in my helmet ear phones. The panel indicated that my number one hydraulic system had failed. We could smell the sweet smell of hydraulic fluid, which had been under 5,000 psi of pressure, which was spraying out into our engine compartment somewhere. The number one hydraulic system powered the helicopter's flight control pedals, collective control along the left side of my seat that controlled the amount power and lift applied to the rotor system, and our hydraulic powered flex weapons systems. We were going to be no good on our mission and procedure was to land as soon as practical.

We happened to be crossing near the Vietnamese air base of Binh Thuy, just north of our base. I called our flight operations and told them of our problem so they could scramble another gunship to replace us, then called the air base control tower for permission to make an emergency landing. Since we were so heavy and had lost most of our rudder and lift control we were not going to be able to make a normal landing stopping at a hover above the ground. Therefore, a run-on landing was planned, much like an airplane, touching down on the runway surface on my skids and skidding to a stop. The collective and rudder pedals would have to be manually forced into position, as much as possible, without the assistance of hydraulic power. A successful run-on emergency landing was made, stopping the helicopter off the main runway on a taxiway so we wouldn't block the runway to other jet fighter traffic. It was a type of emergency landing that we had trained for and practiced many times.

Our gunships had two hydraulic systems, a primary number one system and a number two backup system that doubled up powering the primary cyclic flight control. The cyclic flight control system is the most important because it controls our direction of flight, with turns left and right, and airspeed by pulling back to slow down and by pushing forward to speed up. It's the classic flight control stick between your knees. Our other collective and pedal flight controls were powered by the number one system only. As an added emergency back up, the helicopter was designed with a pressurized nitrogen bottle plumbed into the hydraulic systems to be used if we lost both number one and number two systems. If we lost both hydraulic systems in flight in this C Model gunship, all flight control systems would freeze up and could not be moved. We would simply continue to fly based on where the flight controls were last set. That would be an interesting experience but not one would ever want to encounter. If both hydraulic systems were lost, the nitrogen system could then be switched on to get another few seconds of control movement helping to make a safe landing. The nitrogen backup was a last option for making an emergency landing without crashing.

We had just one little issue with our nitrogen boost system on our gunships in Vietnam. Since we were flying in a combat zone where a lot of bad things were occurring anyway, and due to the difficulty in servicing the nitrogen, the nitrogen bottles had been removed from all gunships. If we lost both hydraulic systems we would experience complete loss of control and would crash. The risk was small compared to the other normal risks flying in our combat environment. So we always flew without that last emergency option if we lost both hydraulic systems in flight. It was a rare occurrence after all.

After our emergency landing this day at Binh Thuy, our maintenance people drove the five miles over to look at the problem. We stuck around to ride back with them. They informed me soon after looking at where the hydraulics had failed, that we had blown both our number one and two systems. The seals had blown out of one of our main cyclic hydraulic actuators in our primary flight control system. Our number one hydraulic system had emptied of fluid first and our number two system was almost out of fluid. If we had continued to fly, we would soon have had another emergency warning indicating that our number two hydraulic system also failed. At that point, our controls would have frozen up. Without knowing it at the time we had landed with fifteen or twenty seconds of semi controlled flight left, maybe less. If we had been a few seconds later getting on the ground all of our controls would have frozen and we would have simply been passengers riding to the scene of our crash. It would have been the ultimate helpless feeling, I expect.

Many times I've wondered what might have been done to try to minimize the impact of a crash in this situation. The throttle in manual control could have been used to change engine torque offering some small amount of directional control. We would have experimented with other things to try to control our flight attitude. We certainly would have dropped our rocket pods and dumped other munitions to reduce our weight. There wouldn't have been many options. The Army Aviation Pamphlet, a magazine sent to all the U.S. Army worldwide, recognized me for a job well done for making a successful landing under extreme emergency conditions. At the time the close call we had wasn't that big a deal. We were lucky.

Heading up north for a mission briefing on similar morning, another interesting maintenance related problem occurred. We had reached three or four thousand feet of altitude and were flying along at one hundred fifty miles an hour with a beautiful sunrise off to the east, when suddenly there was a loud boom. The helicopter yawed severely left and right, then continued on flying normally as if nothing had happened. Immediately checking all my instruments on the instrument panel everything looked normal. I called on the intercom back to my crew asking them what had happened. No one knew, so I asked them to lean out each side and take a look around. My crew chief immediately came back on the intercom and said, "Sir, we've lost all of our engine and transmission cowling."

This was a very dangerous thing to have happen in flight. The cowling that had come off was a heavy double-sided contoured metal part of the aircraft that was about six feet wide by about six feet long. It fit around the main rotor drive shaft, the push-pull control tubes, as well as the engine inlet filter screen assembly, and covered the engine and main transmission. It had ripped off in flight in what would likely have been one large piece. The severe yaw in flight occurred when this large piece of cowling went up through the rotor system and got cut up by the rotor blades. To say this was a dangerous event is a gross understatement. We could have broken off a main rotor blade, disabled our flight controls, or had our tail rotor ripped off as the cowling departed up and away. Any one would have resulted in a catastrophic crash.

Oh well, all's well that ends well. We were lucky, again. We actually flew on to Vinh Long, reported our problem to the helicopter maintenance unit there, and had another cowling assembly installed on our gunship. We, of course, inspected our gunship carefully after this incident, then went on to fly the missions for the day, something we probably should not have done in this gunship without a more detailed inspection.

Yet another experience that was more fun began from the same sort of morning take off into the sunrise. Our mission this day was out west in the mountains supporting the Special Forces again. It was another beautiful, cool, sunny morning, and after turning left around to the west, I decided to make the hour-plus flight to the mountains at low altitude over the broad expanse of rice paddies, characteristic to the area. We were flying about ten feet off the ground with the mountains in the distance, lit by the sunrise behind us. It was a beautiful sight on a beautiful morning. All you could see to the left and right was rice paddy, from horizon to horizon, a huge area.

After a while, a lone figure came into view up ahead. He was hoeing the rice which was growing above the water-covered rice paddy. As we got closer he continued to hoe. We were coming up from behind him at one hundred fifty miles per hour, staying low over the rice. When we got right up to him, he finally realized that some strange, loud noise was upon him. He suddenly turned around, very obviously shocked at what he saw, dropped his hoe and dove into the water as we flew overhead. I remember thinking, *the poor guy. He didn't have to go far to clean out his shorts. We no doubt made his day, maybe his week, or maybe even his year.* How one person could be out in the middle of tens of thousands of acres of rice, hoeing by hand, continues to baffle me to this day. What could possibly be going through a person's mind in this situation, what would he be thinking all day long? No other people were around the area, no village. Maybe he was born into the work on the south side of this vast area and would die when he got to the north side. His life's work.

We were heading west toward the mountains another time, when I got a call to divert from this mission and go look for a Mohawk that had crashed. The Mohawk was a high performance twin turboprop intelligence-gathering airplane. *I had wanted to fly this airplane when first going into the military.* We were given map coordinates of where the plane might have gone down. This information was known since another plane had been flying with it. A crash recovery team was on the way, by helicopter, and we were going to try to locate the downed plane for them before they arrived, then provide gun cover while they worked.

Upon arriving in the area where the crash was supposed to have occurred, we couldn't see any evidence of a crash. No smoke, no aircraft, nothing. The area was a large open area of wet rice paddies near the mountains over near the Cambodian border. We circled around in a continually expanding circle and still didn't find anything. I then decided to take my gun team up to three or four thousand feet to see if we could see anything from higher up. From that altitude, it didn't take long to identify a large pockmark in the otherwise consistent muddy rice paddy surface. There was no airplane or any parts of an airplane visible above ground, just this mark on the surface. It was the only possible location of a crash that could be seen. I called on the radio to the people coming in on the rescue helicopter and reported what we found. We waited around to provide air cover for the recovery team who would land near the site and begin doing their work to locate the aircraft and its occupants.

As the recovery team arrived on site we had further radio contact and I directed them to the specific location of the possible crash. They landed and began digging around in an attempt to confirm that this was the aircraft that was reported crashed. After an hour or so we got a call from the recovery team reporting that it was in fact the crashed aircraft. The aircraft was in many pieces, all under ground level. It had not been a gentle crash. After digging around they found parts of the airplane and pieces of the observer, but could not find any identifying parts of the pilot. They finished their investigative work and, after a while, we all departed the area.

Later in a written report, I read details of the crash investigation. It seems the pilot was taking one of his unit sergeants out flying on a recon mission and was returning to base in Saigon. The pilot had apparently been showing off some and was coming out of a loop, an aerobatic maneuver that was easily done in this aircraft. He may have entered the loop at too low an altitude and on the backside of the loop, heading straight down, hit the ground. He could have been doing over three hundred miles an hour in this fast airplane. The crash scene certainly suggested a high speed impact. The pilot and observer certainly never felt a thing. It would have been a final, quick *oh shit* moment. All pilots need to be conservative and all times and use good sense when flying. That's how one stays alive.

We had a young Warrant Officer gunship pilot in my unit that I had to talk to a couple of times about using good judgment. He was a very good pilot, no question about that, but he needed to make better choices at times. Occasionally, he thought it was fun to stop his 12,000 pound gunship at a hover over a grass hooch and set it down, crushing in the roof. He thought there might have been bad guys inside. He then would take off, blowing the roof off when he pulled full power. Our rotor blast had the force of hurricane winds. He did other things, at times, that were more risky than necessary when working a mission. He was a bit of a cowboy and cowboys sometimes ended up in trouble when flying.

This same guy also kept a record of his kills on a marker board above his bed. He had been there a couple of months less than I had, and had 450 kills marked on his board. *Pleasant dreams!* I didn't need to keep this sort of record. His name prompted an interesting nickname. Upon coming into our unit he was quickly given the nickname Anus. We used his nickname sometimes when we had radio communication with him on missions during lighter moments. We had some chuckles, as did he.

One of our gun pilots used especially poor judgment that cost him his flying career in the military. The pilot and his crew had been using white phosphorous grenades to start fires on the missions they were flying. We often burned hooches, dry rice, dry jungle and other things we wanted to destroy on missions. As they were flying back home that day, they flew over a small village. Someone from the gunship dropped a white phosphorous grenade on the village. This was a particularly nasty thing to do and the pilot, as aircraft commander, authorized the action and was responsible.

When a white phosphorous grenade explodes, the phosphorous powder is spread over a large area and begins to burn as soon as it is exposed to oxygen. It cannot be extinguished by any conventional means, since the burning is a chemical reaction. It is especially nasty when the phosphorous gets on people. It will burn through clothing and into skin and flesh until the chemical reaction stops. Trying to wipe it off just makes it worse. It cannot be extinguished. It has to burn itself out. We seldom used white phosphorous grenades directly on the enemy, and would certainly not expose friendly people to it. It might be considered a form of chemical warfare. Friendly Vietnamese in this little village could have been terribly burned or killed.

There was an inquiry into the incident and the pilot was hauled before a flight review board. He lost his flight status and was stripped of his wings. This is serious for a military pilot. A pilot usually does not get his flight status back after losing it, especially for some serious infraction. This individual was transferred out of our unit. He was no longer a pilot. He could have been given a gun and sent out on foot with an infantry unit. Not a good way to finish a tour in Vietnam.

CHAPTER 13

SPECIAL FORCES ACTION

By September, we began to frequently pull missions over west along the Cambodia border, in and around the mountains that rose up to an altitude of three or four thousand feet. The flying was fun and the country beautiful. We often supported a Special Forces unit that had a small base in that area. The base camp was perhaps ten or fifteen acres with thirty or forty Special Forces guys living there. There was an area inside the barbed wire compound to land our gunships. The lift ships from our unit were normally not there with us. We were there to provide air to ground fire support. Sometimes a C&C ship was along with us to fly Special Forces commanders overhead. We were simply flying in support of Special Forces teams on the ground, usually in or close to the mountains. Our support was in typical form, flying snoop and poop out ahead of a team of guys or flying overhead providing close-in cover and air support. We had to be extremely careful how and where we delivered our weapons fire. We talked directly with commanders on the ground, on our FM radios, and took direction from them as to how to support them and where to direct our weapons fire. They would usually identify their positions with smoke grenades of some color that they would call out and we would confirm. Charlie also had some of our smoke grenades and they were known to also throw smoke, to try to confuse us or lure us into a trap. They were usually hiding, however, when the gunships were around. It was great duty supporting the Special Forces in a beautiful area near the mountains. I loved it.

We were on standby at this base one afternoon when we were called out on an emergency mission. It seems that a Special Forces patrol of eight or ten guys was pinned down up in the mountains by automatic weapons fire from Charlie, while other bad guys were moving around and surrounding them. Charlie was not coming for afternoon tea. The Special Forces guys and Charlie had been in close contact near a ridgeline on the side of a mountain. The overall Special Forces commander was in a command and control ship flying about five thousand feet overhead where he could see and control the operation. He called me on the radio, late in the afternoon, frantic. He needed us to put down covering fire fast, at just the right location, so his guys could run and get away from a badly deteriorating position. The commander was describing some terrain features on the ridgeline to me trying to tell me specifically where to put our rockets. It was hard for him to identify a specific target. Trees, rocks, and cliffs all looked very similar.

I finally thought I saw the spot he was describing. Needing to move quickly, I told him I would make a rocket run and fire one spotter rocket so he could confirm or move the location. One rocket was fired and it impacted a rock outcropping that looked like the right place. At the point of impact and explosion of the rocket the, commander began yelling "That's it, hit it, hit it, hit it!" Because we were fairly early into the run, I had time to fire another three or four rockets. My wingman was right behind me with his rockets impacting on the same spot as we pulled away. The commander immediately called his guys on the same FM radio frequency and began yelling at them to *run, run, run, down the mountain!* They all got away before being completely surrounded by the VC. If that had happened our guys would certainly have all been killed.

Their commander was overjoyed with our performance. He was one happy guy. He would request us specifically in the future to support them. It was really gratifying to feel that we helped some American Special Forces guys live to see another day.

The rocket attack that day was interesting. We flew our dive on target, down quite low to the ridgeline, then banked hard left and flew off the edge of the ridge into open space, two thousand feet or so above the ground. We then pulled up and climbed back to altitude to make another run on the target. Our rocket strikes, in a wide variety of situations, were challenging and really fun. As aircraft commander, rockets were about the only weapon system that I fired. And I got pretty good. I even learned to make a rocket turn a corner, left or right, after launching. This trick was often used to our advantage.

Our sister unit who lived next to us on base didn't do so well one day, when they were supporting the same Special Forces. The unit was the same type unit that we were, in the same battalion, who flew the same sort of missions with lift ships and gunships. Their gunships, on one particular day, fired into the wrong place, hitting some Special Forces guys. One American platoon leader, a lieutenant, was killed and a few other Americans were wounded. A friendly fire incident. This was dangerous business, and how things turned out on missions depended heavily on the skill of individuals, both on the ground and in the air. Some individuals were better at their jobs than others. This is always the case in any line of work, of course, but one mistake in this business could result in deadly consequences. The Special Forces in this area refused to work with our sister unit after this experience. As a result, we flew for them more, which I liked. But we had to be very careful.

Another time we were again working an area to the west over near the mountains. We were scouting an area for a ground operation when we happened upon twenty or so North Vietnamese Army troops, both men and women. We had clearance to engage anyone in this area, near Cambodia, who we could reasonably confirm as the enemy, whenever we found them. These people all had on the distinctive NVA black shirts and pants with reed hats. Some of them were carrying weapons, not a good thing to do in broad daylight. This was a larger group than we normally came across. There was a lot of infiltration of weapons and personnel in this area from the Ho Chi Minh Trail out of Cambodia. We marked up twenty more kills on our windshield and included it in our after action report when we returned home. It was a good day. We killed some more communist enemy.

One day we were working out of a military base near Soc Trang that was down south of us some one hundred miles or so. Our mission was simply to put rocket strikes into a designated area of jungle all day long. The area was near the base and was used by the VC to hide, and from which they staged night mortar attacks. We would rearm and refuel when necessary at the base then fly back out to the strike area and deliver our rocket attacks, firing all our rockets in three or four passes.

While parked on base during a rearming stop with the crew loading rockets, the helicopter began to hop up and down uncontrollably. The engine was at flight idle with a greatly reduced rotor speed and the helicopter was almost hopping off the ground, something it was definitely not supposed to be doing. Obviously, something was really wrong. After rearming, I brought the engine and rotor speed back up to normal operating rpm, lifted up and checked our flight controls at a hover. All seemed normal, so I took off and went out for another rocket attack. Our dives on target started from about four thousand feet. We would reach a hundred sixty miles an hour during a dive, pull out with considerable stress on the rotor system, then climb back up to altitude for another run. After firing all our rockets, with no problems, we went back to base for more rockets and additional fuel. While in refueling at flight idle, the helicopter began to hop up and down again.

We were nearing the end of our workday and there was a helicopter maintenance unit at this base, so I decided to have this checked out. It might not be safe to fly. After refueling and bringing the engine and rotor system back up to full operating rpm, I reported to my gun team what I was doing, and hovered over to the maintenance ramp. Calling to maintenance, we asked them to come out and check out the problem. They sent out a maintenance inspector who turned out to be a Tech Rep from Bell Helicopter in Texas. I explained what the helicopter was doing and he went to work checking it out.

After half an hour or so the inspector reported to me that we had a cracked rotor blade grip. The blade grip is what holds the rotor blade on to the main rotor shaft. The crack extended almost the full length of this critical high strength part. This was a very unusual fracture. A single rotor blade on a Huey weighs two hundred seventy five pounds and the rotor system rotates at about three hundred ninety rpm at operating speed. The blade grip is a heavy alloy steel part that is generally round about two feet long and about eight inches in diameter. There was considerable stress on this part in flight, especially when we were diving on rocket attacks and pulling out. We were lucky not to have had a major structural failure in flight that day. Needless to say, a helicopter drops like a rock without rotor blades.

The helicopter was immediately grounded and determined not flyable. We hitched a ride home on another helicopter. Our unit operations back on our base called the Chinook heavy lift company to go down and carry our gunship back to base, something that had become all together too commonplace. My guardian angel was with us again it seems.

Another morning after flying west over near the mountains for a mission briefing, we had another serious problem. After we shut down, and as I was getting ready to go over to the mission briefing, our crew chief was conducting a post flight inspection. We always did a thorough post flight inspection of all vital parts and systems of the helicopter after every flight to confirm that all systems were operating properly. As the crew chief was climbing up on top of the helicopter to inspect the rotor system he grabbed a hold of one of our two push-pull tubes that connect directly to our two rotor blades. One end of this critical part broke off clean in his hand. He couldn't believe his eyes. These are heavy tubes about two inches in diameter and about three feet long that transfer pitch control to each rotor blade from the swash plate, a rotating plate that transfers angle changes to each rotor blade. To say they are necessary to controlled flight is a real understatement. If it had broken in flight we most certainly would have lost the ability to control the helicopter. Not a good deal. Luckily it broke on the ground so all was okay, again. I took a gunship from one of my wingmen and continued the mission. Yet another gunship to be hooked back home.

About now a strange thing was taking place in our unit. Some guys who had completed their one year tour in our unit, and who had left right after I got there, were returning. Talking to a couple of them, I asked why they had come back. It seems they had an unpleasant time trying to return to the normal routines of civilian life stateside, got really bored and antsy, and didn't like where they were or what they were doing. So they volunteered to return to Vietnam requesting assignment to their previous unit. This very feeling would become a bit of an issue for me later, after my own return home. The excitement of combat action is addicting and the bonds formed with other pilots and crew were very special. We very much became addicted to the action and the adrenaline rush we experienced in combat. There is nothing to equal it back stateside, and to be cut off abruptly requires real adjustment. The abrupt change in returning home was something that was uncomfortable for a lot of guys and many didn't deal with it well.

One thing that was unique and new for me in this combat experience were the bonds that developed between fellow pilots, aircrew and with other military people in Vietnam. The camaraderie between men in life and death pursuits created really strong relationships. It was a unique and very real closeness, but strangely kept at arm's length. We always had to be prepared mentally to lose friends and coworkers on any given day and never see them again. No relationship stateside equaled it, not even a marriage relationship. This sort of relationship was very special.

We didn't necessarily have to know the other guy very well, or even know his name, but we felt close somehow. When an Air Force or Navy pilot would call with an emergency, having taken enemy fire or had some other flight emergency and would be ejecting, Army helicopter pilots nearby would immediately stop their current activity and go to rescue the pilot. We all would fly down the barrels of enemy guns to rescue a downed fellow pilot if needed. One night we had a pilot from our unit fly some distance out into the South China Sea to pick up a Navy pilot who had ejected and parachuted into the sea after having some problem. Our guy flew miles out over open water in the dark, picked up the pilot, hovering nearly in the water, then flew the downed airman back to safety.

Being our Awards and Decorations Officer, I submitted an official recommendation that our pilot be awarded the DFC, Distinguished Flying Cross, one of the highest medals a pilot can get. He never received it though, even after returning stateside.

No word was ever received back from Battalion regarding my recommendation for his medal. I became quite disgusted with the whole situation. The lack of response must have been due to an uncaring or incompetent higher command. Maybe our pilot's rank was not high enough. He was a Warrant Officer. Although following up on my recommendation repeatedly there was no apparent action. As a result, I lost some faith in higher command and administrative political red tape. Along with a number of other experiences in Vietnam, this situation caused me to develop some lasting negative attitudes toward politics and self-serving higher ranking staff officers and politicians. All war time may be the same.

CHAPTER 14

AGENT ORANGE AND FRANK

In October, I was promoted to the rank of Captain. It was common practice at the end of a workday that the individual being promoted would stand in the middle of a large circle of fellow pilots with full buckets of water. On someone's signal they all threw the water on the one being promoted. We did this for all promotions of pilots in our unit. It was likely intended as a substitute for being thrown in the swimming pool at Ft. Rucker. After this dunking we would all go to the officers' club for a few drinks. The newly promoted officer paid the tab. Even though I wasn't a big drinker, the tab was still mine. One beer was the normal limit of my indulgence. Promotion to Captain didn't cause any change in my duties flying or in other duties in my unit on the ground. A pay rise was about the only change which of course is always welcome. Two silver bars now adorned my uniform on each shoulder instead of just one.

A couple of times during the year each of us was given a Red Cross package. It included miscellaneous items like toothpaste, toothbrush, chewing gun, sewing kit, etc. I don't remember what all. It wasn't real significant but the thought was appreciated.

Another time, I received a large box from stateside. It was a real surprise. Originally it had been about fifteen inches square, but all the corners were beat in so thoroughly that the box was almost round. It was about the size of a basketball. It had obviously traveled a long distance and had been handled many times. It's amazing it made it to me at all out in the boonies, halfway around the world.

After some real interest and curiosity about what it was, I opened the package. It turned out being a box of homemade cookies from some ladies at a small church east of Delton, Michigan, my home state. Their name was barely readable on the outside of the box and I don't recall a note inside. The box was full of cookie crumbs and paper towels mixed together. There was no longer any part of a cookie larger than a quarter. For a couple of mornings, my hooch mates and I sat around our hooch, with our morning coffee made over a Sterno stove, eating peanut butter cookie crumbs with large cooking spoons. The "cookies" were good and it was a small touch of home. I regret that I was not able to send them a thank you note. I don't remember a readable return address or any note. Maybe we ate it.

We had some more exposure to Agent Orange near Can Tho. One spray mission, planned for a several day period, took us just south of our base to an area of jungle along both sides of a long canal. There were VC bunkers on both sides of the canal and we were going to burn the leaves off the trees with the nasty orange chemical, eliminating their protection from the hot sun. Defoliating was an activity that the VC, the NVA, and really all other Vietnamese, really detested. They hated it and responded every way they could during our spray operations. I was scheduled to fly the next three days. A wingman would be flying behind me while I flew gun lead behind the spray ship. It was expected to be a dangerous Agent Orange spray operation.

We began the operation flying on the treetops at a higher air speed than was normal for spraying, because it promised to be such a hot area with a lot of enemy fire. Pucker factor was at the max. Each spray run we made was hot from the moment we descended to just above the trees receiving heavy fire from AK 47s. In short, we got our asses shot off. We flew this mission three days in a row starting in the morning, and each day by noon our aircraft was so heavily damaged by enemy fire that we had to cancel the mission for the rest of the day so our maintenance people could make repairs. Why no one among my crew was hit after three days, including me, I don't know.

Since I was not scheduled to fly the fourth day, another pilot, and a friend, Captain Frank B., took my place in the lead gunship. It was not a good day for Frank and his crew. On their first run down over the trees a bullet came through Frank's side window and he was hit in his neck. His jugular veins were severed. He bled to death in a few seconds, as he was being given emergency aid by his crew in the back of the helicopter. Frank's copilot flew as fast as possible at full power to a field medivac hospital, a MASH unit, near our base. Frank bled to death lying on the floor in the back of his gunship while on the way. His blood flooded the floor, soaked into the interior parts of the helicopter, and streaked back along the tail outside as they were flying. It was a real mess. Our maintenance people scrubbed the helicopter, inside and out, with soap and hot water several times, but could not completely rid the aircraft of the smell of blood. I flew this helicopter several times after Frank's death with that special sickening smell. Recall of the smell of this blood-soaked helicopter would stick with me for many years after returning home. Frank will always be remembered. *Rest in peace, my friend.*

Frank was on his second tour to Vietnam. He was an infantry platoon leader during his first tour and was wounded and awarded the Purple Heart. On the night prior to Frank's last day, at the officers' club with some friends, Frank suddenly became very quiet and told the other pilots he was sitting with that he had a very strong feeling that his number was about up. He felt he wasn't going to live much longer. *This information was related after his death.* It's interesting what the human mind can sometimes sense in advance. He died about twelve hours later. Frank's copilot and crew were really shaken up by this experience. The doctors who looked at Frank at the field hospital said he probably could not have been saved even if he'd been shot right on the operating table. He went quickly, a good way to go if you have to I suppose.

It was another sunny day, late in the afternoon, in South Vietnam. Positioning my gunship at an altitude of three thousand feet above my target, I was in a steep dive, launching rockets as fast as the trigger could be pulled. My target was a long canal with palm trees on both sides where the Viet Cong were hiding in tunnels. This is where Frank was shot and killed a few days before. We were delivering some extra punishment on the Viet Cong in this deadly area. I fired twenty rockets before reaching our maximum airspeed and had to begin pulling out of the dive. In the back, my gunners were firing their M60 machine guns continuously. I turned hard left into a steep turn climbing back up to altitude for another rocket strike.

Reaching altitude and performing a wingover maneuver, we rolled back on target in another steep dive. I launched another eighteen rockets in the few seconds it took to reach maximum airspeed. We made another hard left turn and began climbing to altitude heading back to base, when all of a sudden there was a loud explosion. The gunship shuddered and the cockpit filled with white smoke. The enemy in this area reportedly had B40 shouldered fired rockets, like RPG's, so we were always wary and watching for the threat. We were hit hard and I felt the blast on the back of my legs. Immediately, I reduced power and headed down to the ground, our ultimate refuge. Moving my flight controls around on the way down, I could tell that they were still functioning. A quick scan of the gauges on my instrument panel indicated that all systems were operating normally. *Interesting.* Power was applied, stopping our descent and we successfully resumed our climb to altitude and back toward base. Reaching down to check my legs for injury, not knowing immediately how serious a wound there might be, I didn't find anything. I was apparently okay. With a quick survey of the helicopter, a hole was discovered about the size of a softball through my lower door, about a foot away from my seat. There were ragged torn metal edges around the hole. We continued on back to base and landed safely, not knowing for sure what happened.

After some inspection and questioning of my crew, it turned out that my own gunner, sitting behind me in the back, had placed his hot M60 machine gun on the floor after heavy firing, with the barrel pointed forward under my seat. This was something he had been trained, and warned, to never do. His gun had a hot barrel and it cooked off, or fired, a round. The bullet hit a ten pound CO2 fire extinguisher attached to the side of my seat, causing it to explode. The cockpit filled with white CO2 gas and the fire extinguisher blew out through my door. It was a powerful explosion. I was glad the fire extinguisher hadn't hit my legs. It could have caused a major injury. My first thought was that we were not hit by a rocket luckily. It was an accident, but still another close call. One of my own crew almost shot me. This gunner was known to be one of our unit potheads. *That's a good combination, a pothead, with a machine gun, sitting behind me on a mission.* However, this was one of our lesser risks, so no specific issue was made of the incident. No harm, no foul.

A few weeks later, Frank's copilot was called to Saigon to identify Frank's body. Frank was in a cooler at Graves Registration and, somewhere along the line, his identification tag had been lost. He was reportedly lying on a shelf, stiff, an unidentified item of inventory. He was still in his flight suit and hadn't even been cleaned up yet. This was a bad experience for his copilot and friend. They had often flown together. This is an experience one likely does not ever recover from.

We all grieved for Frank for a time of course, knowing that we all faced the same danger every day. I found Frank's name one time on *The Wall* in Washington, along with some other guys I had known. Every wake-up is a good day.

I have fond memories of Frank. We occasionally flew missions together and there is one mission that stands out in particular. We were supporting the Special Forces again over near the Cambodian border. It was early evening. A Special Forces team had been pursuing some NVA across an open area of rice paddies. The bad guys took cover and set up a defensive position in a small stand of jungle in the middle of the open area. As the Special Forces guys approached and came within range, the NVA opened up on them with a machine gun. There was no good cover, only crouching down behind a dike line. They were pinned down. The NVA kept them pinned down so they couldn't move to a different location. It was getting late and our guys didn't want to get stuck there over night. We were called to go help. Talking with the team leader on the ground who explained the situation, our target was identified, the small patch of jungle from which they were being pinned down. Frank was flying my wing.

We planned our strike and climbed to four thousand feet to begin our rocket attack in a medium angle dive. Immediately upon starting the first run, we began taking fire from the NVA machine gun, probably a tripod mounted .30 caliber. We could tell from the steady stream of accurate fire coming up at us. The green tracer bullets (communist) came up and passed all around us, above, below, left and right. The bad guys gave away their location and pinpointed the target since we could see muzzle flashes from their machine gun.

As we were in our dive, firing rockets, the green tracers kept coming up around us as we got closer and closer. It was exciting and more than a little spooky. A bullet that was not a tracer bullet and was invisible could have come through our windshield at any moment. At the end of my dive on target, I pulled out hard to the left and Frank had his rockets impacting the target area to cover my turn away and climb back to altitude. During his run Frank, was on the radio yelling, "Yeeeee haaaa whoooooo!" He was having a ball. It was exciting, almost like right out of a WWII movie. On my next run I adjusted my rocket fire and dropped several rockets right on top of the bad guys. We both got direct hits on the machine gun and it stopped firing, so we stopped the attack. It's nice when you can hit your target.

It would have been great to be able see what was left of the machine gun position on the ground and the effect from our rockets. Luckily we didn't take any hits. Our Special Forces guys stood up and walked back to their base. The Special Forces team leader called me on the radio to say thanks. Frank died just a few weeks later.

CHAPTER 15

GIRLS AND GUNS

We had an Australian girls' show scheduled to come to our officers' club, organized by the USO. Girls with round eyes were considered a real treat. Since I scheduled flight duty for our gunship pilots, I decided to schedule myself and a few friends down on the day of the show. So we flew more in the days before the show to do our part. To make sure we got good seats at the club we went early, arriving around three o'clock in the afternoon. We got a big table right up near the stage that had been set up for the show. The club was serving all you can eat spaghetti and we started eating and drinking beer. The show was to start at eight o'clock. We had a lot of time to kill so we continued to eat and drink at a slow pace. Not being much of a drinker and drinking a little more than normal, it went to my head a little bit. The place filled up with other officers as it got close to show time.

The show was finally introduced. The music started and out came a troop of eight tall, pretty, round-eyed girls, all dressed in pink ostrich feathers and bikinis. A real pretty sight, after looking at comparatively unattractive Vietnamese and olive drab green for a long time. The show went on for a couple of hours with singing and dancing to a number of popular tunes. At one point, I stood up and yelled out something nice to the girls, which was totally uncharacteristic of me. It got their attention and we got some friendly waves. It was a nice show. After the show we all piled into a jeep and made our way back to our unit on the corner of the base, maybe a mile away. I was sick for a couple days from the excess beer drinking and vowed to never do that again.

There were other, non-sanctioned, shows from time to time. of the not-so-nice variety. Some were down right gross so we heard. They were usually in some warehouse near the main gate. It sounded rather disgusting and I never went.

One evening at Dong Tam, our previous base, our sister unit who was based right next to us on the airfield put on a special show that they had planned. It was a strip show with Vietnamese girls. Our unit was invited and many of the guys went. From later reports, it was a fairly decent show, with guys invited on stage to untie bikini tops and bottoms with their teeth. The music was okay and the crowd of guys were whooping and hollering. The music and all the hoopla was easily heard from my location nearby.

Later in the middle of the night long after the show was over, we came under another mortar attack. Call it what you want but that night was not a lucky night for our sister unit that held the party. Their operations shack, only fifty yards away from us, took a direct hit from a mortar round. The company commander and a couple other officers were inside. The company commander, a major, was killed and the others wounded. I was asleep in my hooch nearby. It would have more appropriate if the mortar round had landed on one of the less nice shows somewhere else. Charlie should have been more selective.

Girls, for a lot of guys in Vietnam, were a big deal as you might imagine. I had a specific offer from another officer one time to join what was an *exclusive club*. Some select officers, it seems, could schedule time with a Vietnamese girl off base, downtown in Can Tho. The girls were reportedly set up in a nice place that was maintained by the military, unofficially of course. It was certainly a for-profit venture, at least for the girls. They supposedly had regular medical check-ups from our doctors.

Some military guys were probably making a little extra money on the side, as well. Managing this *club* could well have been an extra duty assigned to an officer from some other *suppor*t unit. The U.S. military takes care of its own overseas, in many ways that are not officially reported or talked about. I wonder sometimes about what we don't hear, related to the more recent Middle East conflicts. We don't need to know.

Although not disinterested, I never pursued any *extra curricular* activities with girls while in Vietnam. We all heard stories that were not pretty. We had to attend a mandatory lecture shortly after arriving in Vietnam, presented by military doctors, regarding contracting all sorts of diseases, and how to try to avoid them. They gave us practical information, knowing that many guys were going to get involved with the girls. The doctors also related stories concerning some guys over there who had contracted strange diseases that would not respond to any medical treatment. After a while, if the doctors could not identify and cure a disease, the afflicted were sent away to places unknown for a hopeful cure. Supposedly, there were some confidential locations away from Vietnam where guys were sent for treatment and stayed until they got well. They would not be permitted back in the States with unknown, untreatable diseases. Some of those guys could still be listed among the official missing in action today.

Many things that occurred in Vietnam were not reported factually to family, or others, back in the States. Strange things can and do happen in a large military organization overseas in a combat zone and sometimes family and friends are protected with more favorable reports. Information couldn't always be confirmed as factual, but as a commissioned officer information was often provided from fairly reliable sources. But we never had all the information or all the facts. No one did. Just like today. We should be content that we sometimes don't know everything.

I had a wife and little daughter back home and I wasn't going to get involved in activities with girls which would have been very foreign to me anyway. I also likely was a little naïve. Interestingly, there was little interest in those kinds of activities on my part. The intensity and serious nature of my work was a major force in keeping my mind on business. There were larger concerns here. We were quite busy. There also was the feeling that if I was going to die over there, which was a real possibility, I wanted my last thoughts to be of home and good memories, free of any last guilt or bad feeling. If that was to happen, and if there were a few seconds or minutes of thought remaining, I wanted to go peacefully.

My number could have been called anytime. I was resigned to the very real prospect that my life could end before the end of my tour, that I would not return home alive. Mental self-conditioning of this sort would have a long lasting effect on me well into the future.

With only a couple more months to go before my tour was done, I was still having a good time flying and enjoying the sights and smells of this ancient oriental country. A lot of the local people were beautifully dressed in their native attire. Many women on base, and in villages we flew over, wore colorful dresses, while the men dressed simply in loose pants and shirts. Many of them, both men and women, wore the conical-shaped, round reed hat.

My flight routine had me flying an average of four days a week. All days were the same. There were no weekends or weekdays. Almost every day in the air we were shot at and most days we took bullet hits, some close to me and my crew. Our helicopter was routinely patched over night by the maintenance people. They used a two part epoxy type putty to plug the bullet holes, and made other types of mechanical repairs. Earlier in the year much of the enemy fire came from single shot bolt action rifles of Chinese origin. By now, almost all the enemy fire came from AK 47's of Russian origin. They could really work us over in a hurry. The VC were getting better at what they did and were much better equipped.

Early in my tour, I had figured out specific actions in flight that would offer maximum protection to my crew, myself and to the aircraft when we came under enemy fire. These actions would serve us well as the year worn on. The basic logic was that my crew was most important and they should be protected as a first priority. The aircraft also ranked a close second in my priorities, since it was our ride home. A ride home is always a good thing. If we were caught by surprise, by enemy fire, especially at low altitude, I would immediately turn the belly of the helicopter to the fire, placing what armor we had between us and them and quickly fly away. I would then fly to a more desirable position, turn back on the enemy and unload on them. This tactic worked well. It's not something we were taught specifically. Some things we simply learned from experience and applying common sense. Protecting my crew was a very big thing for me.

My reputation among our crewmen was that of a competent and safe pilot to fly with. Conservative in my flying, I used good judgment and first and foremost protected my crew. I had gained a lot of flying experience by now and knew pretty well how to maintain, perhaps improve, odds for survival in this combat environment. Out of curiosity I kept a record of the last three months that I flew, averaging four days a week. There were only three or four days in those last three months when we returned to base *without* bullet hits in the aircraft. We came under a lot of enemy fire almost every day. The bad guys were trying to kill us. So far we had been real lucky. We had a lot of close calls, but no crew member of mine had been hit nor had I. This was a record that felt really good.

A bullet hit the upper door frame on the left side of our gunship, one day, about six inches from my copilot's left ear. *Do you think they were aiming at him?* It was a very close miss and a memorable day for him. He likely had an extra beer at the *O Club* that evening. I can still picture this fellow pilot, a captain like me, but I don't remember his name. We saw a lot of close-up action. We usually got the upper hand quickly with superior firepower and often eliminated the enemy threat before he could hurt us too bad. Response speed and accuracy was important. We were an experienced, accurate and effective airborne firepower delivery machine. Much of the time the enemy would duck and hide until we flew away. Other times not.

It was a normal part of life over there to make light of the danger we were exposed to regularly. We had to joke about it, and laugh at it, not taking it too seriously or we would not be able to keep our heads on straight and do our jobs. We didn't dwell very long on our near misses and other unpleasant things that occurred. In general, we couldn't take life too seriously. One of our pilots who had some drawing ability drew a Snoopy cartoon for me one time. I have it framed today and hanging in our bunkhouse up in the woods. I don't remember his name. He crashed and died a few months after giving me the cartoon.

We also had a lot of guys who were wounded, flown out by medevac helicopter and were never seen again. Guys remaining, who lived in the hooch with the guy who had departed, were assigned the task of cleaning out and boxing up his personal effects to be sent home. Personal effects were *sanitized* before they were sent home to family. Any *dirty laundry* was thrown out.

Some guys were just unlucky. Luck does have its place, it seems. New pilots into a unit seemed to be especially unlucky for some reason. We had a new Warrant Officer arrive one week, start flying the next week, then took a bullet hit to his crotch the next week. He was sent home by Air Force air ambulance. He most likely lost his manhood. An attack helicopter unit across the airfield from us had a new pilot arrive one day, and the next day he was killed by enemy fire on his first day flying as copilot. He had a short, very bad tour. Only those left behind knew it though.

We normally had a lot of mission flexibility and most of the missions we flew were not all that critical, in my view, since the whole conflict over there was basically political in nature and often appeared rather screwed up. But we did the work we were given. Winning the hearts and minds of the Vietnamese people was not working, however. The American military could not conduct military operations in any area without approval from Vietnamese politicians or local province chiefs. It was pretty common knowledge that many officials were paid off by the NVA or Viet Cong. Threats to the lives of officials and their families by the VC was common and also worked against us. The conduct of our missions was often slanted in favor of the enemy it seemed.

Most American combat operations stopped at night understandably, as it was much more difficult to conduct military operations in the dark. This was when the Viet Cong and NVA emerged as the more effective military force because they could operate under cover of darkness. They were a threat to the U.S. military and they intimidated, and even conducted military action against their own people, especially those who worked with the Americans. It sounds a lot like Iraq and Afghanistan today. Maybe all war is the same. Local civilian populations are often caught in the middle between forces and suffer the most.

Flying cover for the Navy was great duty. We occasionally got missions to cover river operations on smaller rivers and canals. The Navy would motor their small high speed gunboats,

PBR's, up and down rivers and in and out of canals, looking for munitions that were being carried down into South Vietnam in innocent appearing sampans. The large Mekong River flowed into South Vietnam out of Cambodia splitting into two large tributaries before going into the South China Sea. Most of my time flying in Vietnam was around these tributaries. Weapons, people, ammunition and explosives would be transported by boat people who appeared to be simple families going about their daily lives along the river. Men, women, chickens, goats and kids were often on board.

The gunboats didn't take any chances and leaned toward being unforgiving. If they stopped a boat to inspect and they saw any suspect or unusual activity, or perhaps some contraband, they sometimes just shot everything up including all the people. This probably would be an extreme case though. There was a saying in Vietnam that was common among troops who were close to the action, where it was often impossible to tell friend from foe. *Kill 'em all and let God sort 'em out.* This was a common attitude on a lot of combat operations in Vietnam. Women had been known to carry a hand grenade or other explosive in a basket with their babies, then detonate it around American troops. We were inclined not to take unnecessary chances.

I was close, but not real close, to the action on the ground. At arms-length. After we did our dirty work we would usually just fly away to other action. This was a real luxury, if it can be called that, for a pilot. It helped save one's sanity. *Only partly some may say.*

Our mission one afternoon was to cover a river insertion of combat troops where the troops were transported downriver in a Navy landing craft. The boat had a large open hull where the troops were carried and a large gate on the front that dropped down for unloading. The landing craft had an automatic 37 millimeter cannon mounted on the front right corner. As they approached their landing site along a stretch of jungle-covered shoreline, the gunner opened up with the 37 millimeter to soften up the landing. We were circling closely overhead looking for bad guys. It was interesting watching that gun firing. The river landing point was quiet, with no enemy action. After watching the automatic 37 mm cannon firing, it was not surprising.

As the afternoon progressed flying overhead covering the ground action, a sampan with four or five guys in it started paddling quickly across the river, away from the action. They knew better than to show any weapons or to shoot at us. The ground troops considered them the bad guys. They were out-manned and out-gunned. The ground commander, who we had radio contact with, directed us to take them out. We were flying slowly around them at an altitude of perhaps fifty feet. They were sitting ducks, literally. We opened up on them with one of our mini guns. We didn't miss. As our gun roared, the water rose to a hover above and around the boat from the hundreds of bullets impacting. In one momentary span of a couple seconds there was one guy looking up at us, then he melted away. The boat was turned totally to splinters and the river slowly carried away the large red blotch and the pieces of wood. More black marks on our windshield.

We were called out another day to provide gun cover for a Sky Crane extraction. The Sky Crane is the large cargo transport helicopter that looks like a praying mantis. It was the heaviest lift helicopter the military had. It is still used today for heavy lifting by various civilian operators. It seems one Sky Crane had some sort of mechanical trouble in the boonies and made an emergency landing. Another Sky Crane was called to lift it out and back to a secure base. The problem was that one Sky Crane would not lift another unless the two engines were removed, because it would be too heavy. We circled overhead all day, providing gun cover while a maintenance crew removed the engines, which were flown away by another helicopter. They then hooked up the disabled helicopter with a long nylon strap and lifted it up with the second lift helicopter. They carefully lifted it straight up and flew away. It was the maximum weight the lift helicopter could carry. We saw no other action that day. It was rather boring actually.

There were some really unusual and interesting sights, on occasion, during my year flying in Vietnam. One time I had set my helicopter down for a short stop near a small village out in the boonies. The village was small with no obvious roads going anywhere and with small grass huts and shacks. There were no visible electric wires so there was likely no electricity. As we were sitting on the ground with the helicopter running at idle, a small boy ran out from the village up to my door with a canvas bag. He opened the bag and it was full of crushed ice with cold bottles of Coca Cola sticking up, that he was selling. Where on earth did he get the ice and Cokes? It's still a mystery. We had been warned not to drink the local Coka Cola, bottled in Saigon, because it was not pure and had formaldehyde in the formula to kill the bugs. I bought one and drank it anyway. It really tasted great on this hot day. *What was it going to do? Kill me?*

Another time, we were flying along over an open rice paddy at low level. It was warm and sunny and everything around was green. Looking far up ahead, I noticed something orange sticking out in sharp contrast. Curious, I continued ahead to check it out. As we got close it became easily identifiable. It was a fairly new looking Allis Chalmers tractor sitting along side a dike line. It might have been sitting where it ran out of gas. Where did that tractor come from and how did it get there, way out in the middle of nowhere? I never saw another Allis Chalmers tractor anywhere in Vietnam. *Crazy.*

Flying along one time, I noticed a car speeding along up ahead on the top of a dike line. There were often two track dirt roads on the tops of dike lines between rice paddies. We were out in the boonies again, away from a town of any significant size, and it was unusual to see a car. I flew ahead to take a look. There in plain view was a '56 Chevy coupe speeding along with a cloud of dust trailing behind. *Wow!* This sight put a big smile on my face. I'd love to have that car back stateside.

Another day we were operating out of a small stage field with a two thousand foot long PSP steel plank runway surface. We refueled at this small airfield. We had been told to park well away from the runway and shut down our helicopters, because the Air Force would be coming in to deliver fuel. We were curious what sort of plane loaded with fuel could be used on this very short runway, so we sat waiting for the Air Force to arrive. Finally off in the distance we saw a C130 cargo plane heading our way. This small stage field was obviously too small for the large C130 aircraft to land. As the C130 approached he descended to a very low altitude, perhaps 10 feet above the ground, and his large back cargo door opened. As the pilot flew low over the runway, he popped a drogue parachute out the back and with it came a large pallet loaded with 55 gallon drums of jet fuel. The pallet must have been ten feet wide or so by thirty feet long. The pallet dropped the few feet to the runway surface and skidded down the runway, coming to a stop right in front of our refueling area. The C130 had to have been flying 130 miles an hour or so when he dropped his load. It was an amazing thing to see. There were many interesting sights during my year in Vietnam.

October 30th was my birthday. A birthday card or two from home were probably received, but I don't remember. Birthdays in Vietnam were not particularly noteworthy. At twenty-five years old, I was an older guy compared to most. Many of our pilots went to basic training right out of high school, then on to Warrant Officer School where they received some basic officer training and learned to fly. They did not need a college degree. Many pilots were younger guys who were just nineteen or twenty years old. All they were expected to do was fly helicopters after nine months of flight school. I was a commissioned officer, currently a captain, a small unit commander first by official designation, but also a helicopter pilot. A college degree was required to become a commissioned officer through ROTC. So after five years of college, basic officer training, then flight school, I was older than many other of our pilots.

Many young pilots were good pilots and some were not very good. We wondered how some made it through flight school. Most were certainly not in the top of their class and some had to be near the bottom, minimally qualified. As a result, certain pilots only flew copilot and never were advanced to aircraft commander in charge of their helicopter operations. One guy in our gun platoon was a particularly weak pilot and mostly just rode along. Other guys would pick on him sometimes, but he was good natured and went along with it. *We all picked on each other.* One prank was to make him pee all over himself. When we'd be set down on the ground for a few minutes, still running at flight idle on some short delay, some guys would get out of the helicopter walk up front a little way and take a pee. When this guy stepped out front, the pilot still in the helicopter on the controls would occasionally pull a little pitch in the rotor blades creating a strong wind. His pee would fly up in the air all over him. We needed chuckles sometimes. A little humor, even sick humor, countered some of the other more serious stuff going on. I still react to a little sick humor sometimes. Today, however, I tend to be somewhat humorless. It's healthy to laugh we're told.

CHAPTER 16

THANKSGIVING C'RATS

About now it seemed like I'd been in Vietnam nearly forever, a lifetime almost. November was turkey month, Thanksgiving. We were still flying the same sort of highly varied missions. The aerial attack missions where we just pounded some point with rockets were the most fun for me. They were simple, and not a lot of work. Guess I was becoming lazy. We would often start our attack on target from three or four thousand feet, diving at different angles from low angle to high angle, depending on the type of target. We could hit a smaller target on the ground more accurately in a high angle attack, but our dive was shorter in duration because we'd hit our maximum airspeed faster. We chose an attack profile that would yield the most effective strike results. River operations were interesting and the most fun. There were lots of rivers and canals around.

Thanksgiving Day was coming up but nobody made a big deal of it. Charlie didn't have a Thanksgiving Day, of course, but he was probably still thankful he wasn't dead yet. *Go celebrate dude!* Maybe they didn't think such things. The missions were planned to continue on Thanksgiving Day, as usual. Our mess hall promised a good Thanksgiving dinner with turkey and all the fixin's. I flew that day so one of the other guys could have the day off and enjoy the big midday meal that was planned. It was later reported to have been very good.

That day was nothing particularly special to me. I was thankful every day. The mission had us flying all day long and we all had C rations for lunch. One of our crew members would heat his C ration main meal in the exhaust of our jet engine before we shut down for lunch. It came in a can about the size of a Campbell soup can and could be held with a long-handled set of pliers in the exhaust pipe for about thirty seconds. The mysterious food in the can looked, and sometimes smelled, just like canned dog food but it wasn't too bad, if one was hungry. Dog food might have been good too under the circumstances. We often had a hot meal at noon right out of our jet engine tail pipe. This was normal lunchtime routine in the boonies when we had time.

It was a memorable Thanksgiving Day 1969. When we returned to base in the late afternoon we did have leftovers from the main meal, which were good even with a plastic forks and survival knives as our only utensils. Thanksgiving leftovers are still a favorite of mine today. The turkey was great compared to C rats. It was sliced up, no doubt having come over canned from stateside. There were no turkeys anywhere in Vietnam that I had seen. Maybe I wasn't looking close enough. The only *turkeys* were human.

We were flying again over west of Can Tho, simply putting in rocket strikes in an area of jungle. My wingman, nicknamed Cajun, was flying a gunship with the tail number 222. We identified helicopters by their tail numbers. We called this one *triple deuce.* Every helicopter flies a little differently, each with its own unique characteristics, and triple duce had a very weak engine with low power. We all knew this and had to fly it accordingly. When it was heavily loaded with fuel, rockets and other munitions, we had difficulty taking off in triple duce. We would often have to make a running take off skidding along the ground until it built up enough air speed to lift off, almost like an airplane.

Between strikes on this particular day, we refueled and rearmed at a small stage field near our strike target. After one turnaround for more fuel and rockets, I took off. Cajun began his takeoff behind me. Triple duce was heavily loaded. I had just turned to the right after take off and was climbing to altitude when another pilot at the stage field called me on the radio and said, "Copperhead lead, your wing man just crashed." I looked at my copilot and said, "What?" Then it struck me, *CRASHED!* I immediately turned hard left, looked for and saw my downed wingman, and dove toward the open wet rice paddy off the end of the runway.

Cajun's gunship was lying on its left side in the water and mud, all crumpled up with steam rising from it. No crewmembers could be seen. I dove our gunship as fast as I could to the crash site, expecting to have to rescue our guys. As we got closer and closer, four guys rose up out of the mud and water, one at a time. I couldn't believe my eyes. All our guys were walking away through the foot deep water and mud. We came down low and hovered around them. They all looked more or less okay but were obviously shaken up. *Thank you, guardian angel.* They were picked up by another helicopter from the stage field and flown back home to our base.

We flew one more attack on our target then also flew back to base. All of us immediately checked on our guys from triple duce. Cajun and the other crewmembers were a little banged up and limped around for a few days, but were generally okay. Reviewing the crash with Cajun, he told me that he had turned right after take off with low rotor speed and immediately after the turn, the gunship simply quit flying. There's a technical reason why this happened but simply put, there was no way he could hold the gunship in the air. He flew into the ground at around sixty miles an hour. The windshields and all the windows broke out on impact and the bomb rack holding nineteen rockets on the right side broke off. After the helicopter came to a stop, the pilots crawled out through the open windshields. One door gunner crawled out of the mud from under the left side of the gunship after it had rolled over on top of him. They were all quite fortunate.

There would be no recovery of this helicopter. An EOD (Explosives Ordinance Demolition) team went in that evening, planted explosive charges around the gunship, and blew everything up. We couldn't have Charlie getting our rockets and other valuable items off the helicopter. Before the EOD team blew the gunship they took a picture, and later gave it to me. It's included in the photo section of this book.

My work had become quite routine by now. We still had some interesting flying missions though. One night my mission was to simply fly over the top of our base all night long providing gun cover. This was the only time this mission was assigned to me, although someone flew the mission every night. It was real quiet. We had GCA radar on our base. GCA stands for Ground Controlled Approach. We had radio contact with the radar controllers, as well as the control tower at the airfield. Overnights were real boring for the GCA guys working in a trailer next to the runway, so we took advantage of the opportunity to fly several practice GCA approaches. It was good practice for all of us and killed some time.

On final approach to the air field some three miles out, the GCA controllers would take over and talk us right down to about five feet off the ground, within sight of the runway surface. On the radar screen the controllers saw us as a blip, a couple small bright lights, on a horizontal profile screen as well as on a vertical profile screen. On our approach they told us to fly left or right, to stay on course horizontally, or go up or down to stay on the vertical glide path using standard radio communication procedure. Their accuracy when controlling our approach was a foot or two in any direction. This radar service was provided for those bad weather conditions in fog or rain when we would fly an approach to land without being able to see the airport or the ground. Bad weather at night was especially bad because it was so dark. It was really black some nights.

While circling overhead on this particular overnight duty, we would sometimes fly right over the South Vietnamese Army base just north of us. A few times as we passed overhead red tracer bullets came flying up at us. One out of every five bullets is a tracer bullet, so a lot of additional bullets were coming up at us that we couldn't see. The fire was coming from our friendly South Vietnamese Army guys using American M16 combat rifle that American taxpayers were nice enough to provide. *Some thanks!* We were three or four thousand feet up, so they didn't hit us. A bullet is pretty well spent by that altitude, especially the smaller bullet that the M16 fired. My gunship was never hit at that altitude even by an AK47.

Bob, one of my flight school classmates, was stationed up north with another unit and was reportedly killed while flying at an altitude of five thousand feet one day. He was flying in the front seat of a Cobra and was hit by a single round from a Russian .51 caliber. It was just bad luck. The .51 caliber, which was about the same as our .50 caliber, would reach that altitude and beyond. The .51 caliber bullet is about the size of your little finger fully extended. I flew with Bob quite a lot in flight school. We were stick buddies in advanced flight school at Ft. Rucker flying the Huey. He left behind a young wife and a baby daughter, who was born while we were in flight school, just as my daughter was. I was sad to hear upon returning to the replacement battalion on the way home that he had bought it. Bob was a good guy.

Speaking of Russian 51's, one day we were supporting the Special Forces guys over near the Cambodian border at the foot of the mountains. We were shut down and parked on the base on standby ready if they needed us. It was a beautiful sunny day, not too hot. I had a flight of three gunships. Some of the crew and pilots had their shirts off getting some rays, some were eating C rats, some were playing cards or reading. It was a beautiful, quiet, leisurely setting with a cool breeze. Paradise!

All of a sudden we heard some muffled *pop, pop, pop* sounds coming from the side of the mountain next to us, maybe a mile away. It got our attention and we all wondered what it was. A couple of seconds later we heard what can only be described as high speed basketballs flying overhead. A real distinct swishing sound passing overhead fast. A couple seconds later we realized we were being shot at and the fire had to be coming from a Russian .51 caliber machine gun. We were being shot at by North Vietnamese Army regulars from up on the side of the mountain with their most powerful machine gun. They had a beautiful juicy target down below. Us!

Instinctively I ran to my gunship thinking I was going to take off and try to attack them. It took all of about two seconds to realize that I should seek some cover. All of us ran to large revetments lined up where helicopters normally parked overnight, and dove to the ground. It was good cover that blocked us from the enemy fire. The protective barriers were about ten feet tall and some six feet thick filled with dirt. Their sides were facing the mountain where the fire was coming from so it was good protection. As we were hiding behind the revetments, the NVA adjusted their fire, no doubt watching the path of their tracer bullets, and brought their fire down on us. Several rounds hit the revetments that we were hiding behind. Maybe thirty seconds later the firing stopped. We were all okay. When it was safe, we checked our gunships and they too were okay. There were no hits. Charlie must have been aiming at us instead of our helicopters.

While Charlie was shooting at us the Special Forces guys got a fix on his location and called the Air Force for support. The Air Force sent a couple of F4's to hit the side of the mountain. They arrived about five minutes later. They made several runs with 20 millimeter cannon, pounding the spot where the enemy had been. Charlie was no doubt back inside his mountain by then sipping tea and likely not worried even a little bit. It was a great show though seeing the F4's work out with their cannon. The rest of the day was quiet and we didn't go out again. But we kept an eye on the side of that mountain. At the end of our day we flew the hour or so flight back to Can Tho. I mentally logged another interesting experience. It's strange how one can remember this sort of thing so clearly for so long.

Probably five or six times in my year in Vietnam I was assigned on ten minute standby mission overnight with a flight of gunships and crew. This is where we would have our gunships fully loaded with weapons and fuel, and ready to go with most of our start procedure completed. We sometimes waited on the flight line close to our gunships, other times we would be at the operations building in our unit area with a truck ready to take us on a moments notice to the flight line. We were expected to be in the air within ten minutes of a call for support from someone needing help. One pilot would jump in the helicopter and immediately flip the battery switch on and pull the start trigger to get our jet turbine engine started, while the other pilot was strapping on his seat belt and shoulder harness and putting his helmet on. When he was ready he took the start while the other pilot strapped in. We would crank up to operating rpm, do quick operational checks and take off all within ten minutes. We usually didn't do much on these standby missions because nights were normally fairly quiet.

One night though around midnight we got a call for help. I had a team of three gunships. Our mission was to fly due north, up west of Saigon, to help a Special Forces outpost that was being attacked by the bad guys. First, we were to go to a small base near the outpost being attacked, for a mission briefing with local commanders. Prior to taking off I got the mission details quickly from flight operations, did a quick map study and saw that the direction was almost exactly due north and about 140 clicks (kilometers) away.

After takeoff I set my directional gyro to the magnetic compass heading and we started north. We soon realized that we had no moonlight at all. The moon was a sliver at best and we had a high solid overcast. It was dark. Real dark. Picture yourself in a box painted black on the inside with the top on tight. That's what we were flying in. That late at night there were no lights on the ground and we could not see anything. Not the ground, not the horizon, nothing. It was a total black void.

Our flight time would be almost exactly one hour. I told my copilot to take control, stay on the instruments and fly exactly north for one hour. We would then try to find the base we were to go to, that would most likely be blacked out. We literally were flying IFR on instruments, only in perfectly clear weather. I was watching my copilot's flying carefully. There was nothing to see outside. We had no navigational aids or navigational radar over there so we were completely on our own. I was watching the time.

Exactly an hour later we began circling to try to find the base. We still couldn't see anything although we knew we had to be close. We flew down low and turned on our searchlight. It was totally black, almost spooky. We finally flew across some revetments alongside the airstrip and zeroed in on the airfield. Looking around, we finally landed near a refueling point and hovered over to take on some fuel. We had our belly landing light on, which was normal at night while on the ground because it lit up the whole area around the helicopter. At this point we saw something interesting. As we were sitting there refueling, off to my left and not too far away, a pair of bare white butt cheeks were bouncing up and down, close to the ground. It didn't take long to figure out what was going on. One of our pilots who had arrived earlier apparently found a willing Vietnamese girl for a little extra action on the side. This was not an uncommon occurrence day or night. Many Vietnamese girls liked American boys and a little extra money. Money was hard to come by, especially out in the boondocks.

It was still totally black except for the lights on the helicopters. This was a somewhat surreal situation in what turned out to be a somewhat surreal night. After topping off our fuel we hovered over along a road, near a truck trailer that served as command and control for the local forces. We went in for a quick mission briefing. We heard about the Special Forces unit being attacked by the VC. We were to fly out and make contact with the local commander on the ground, review the situation and provide air to ground supporting fire. We went back to our gunships quickly to get cranked up and head out to help our guys. I started my gunship, went through my run up checks and got ready to hover out and take off. My wingmen were doing the same.

As we were sitting there at flight idle I noticed a jeep heading our way. When he got closer I could see a long antenna mounted on the back of his jeep sticking up some twenty feet or so. It was used as a command and control radio. In the rush of battle as they say, he apparently was not thinking clearly, because he drove under my rotor blades as they were spinning around. The rotor blades made quick work of the antenna. It was chopped into a flurry of pieces. *Turkey! Quickly, what to do? Should we go ahead with the mission or take the time to shut down and check our rotor blades for possible damage?* I decided to shut down and take a quick look. This turned out to be a good decision. Upon inspecting the rotor blades, I found a wide gash in one blade, about an inch wide by about fifteen inches long that went all the way through the rotor blade.

Our gunship was immediately grounded. We could not fly safely with this damage. I told my capable wingman to take the mission and get going. The helicopter would have initially flown okay probably but at great risk of soon having the rotor blade break off in flight. That would not have been good. There was nothing else for my crew and me to do at this point but wait. I crawled up on top of the helicopter then up on top of our two foot wide rotor blades laid on my back and studied the stars. The rotor blade was ten feet or so above the ground so it was away from most of the mosquitoes.

When our two remaining gunships came back from the mission, my crew and I got aboard getting a ride back to home base. It turned out that most of the action at the Special Forces outpost was over by the time they got there to help, so the action didn't amount to much. It was sort of a wasted night. On the way back we called to operations and reported that my gunship was grounded. They had a lift company fly up later in the morning and hook it back home, again. *Their job had to be way too much fun.* Having been up all night, I went back to my hooch and hit the sack.

CHAPTER 17

STRANGE HOLIDAYS

December was an interesting month. Santa Claus was coming. *Ho, ho, ho.* We delivered some pretty rocket-fired presents to the VC, all decorated with ugly green paint and nice rocket flame colored ribbon. After Thanksgiving Armed Forces Radio out of Saigon began playing Christmas music on their FM radio frequency. We had multiband FM radios in all our helicopters for communication with ground forces. It was the radio's only use other than listening to Armed Forces Radio. Often, when we were simply flying from point A to point B for a mission briefing or back home after the day was complete, we would tune in to the Armed Forces Radio frequency and listen to music, news, weather and such. All the normal stuff. Sometimes when we were hitting a simple target with rockets or mini guns we would also be entertained with Armed Forces radio tuned in.

As we got closer to Christmas, we began listening to all the traditional Christmas music as we were flying. *Silent Night, Jingle bells, Rudolph the Red Nosed Reindeer,* etc. We often flew low level in the sunny warm weather that had returned after the monsoons, over beautiful green palm trees, quaint little villages with grass huts and thatched roofs with locals out working in their fields, while listening to Christmas music. It could be a very peaceful, quiet setting at times. I enjoyed the beauty of the country and its people at every opportunity. Sometimes I could remove myself for a short time from where we were and what we were doing and just enjoy the moment. In stark contrast, other times we'd be putting in a rocket strike somewhere shooting at bad guys on the run or blowing up and burning hooches while listening to *Peace on Earth, Good Will Toward Men*. It was a bit of a mind bender. It was interesting trying to reconcile our actions with what we were listening to on the radio. It struck me at the time as being quite ironic. Other times we'd be headed out to put in a rocket strike to *Santa Claus is Coming to Town*. Was he ever, with an interesting bag of goodies. It was an interesting time. It was nice listening to the radio during Christmastime 1969.

Armed Forces Radio regularly broadcast along with the normal music, news, and weather what can only be described as a radio cartoon. It was titled *Chicken Man*. He was supposedly a chicken who was a combination warrior, law enforcement officer, and general do-good Superman type. He lived with his mother. *A real chicken man*. He was called The Great White-winged Warrior.

I always pictured a scrawny white leghorn rooster like we used to have back home when I was a kid. We could listen to the adventures of Chicken Man doing good deeds and solving crimes as we flew around. It was rather silly and stupid, like many of today's TV commercials, but it was mildly entertaining. They were short three or four minute pieces and were played a few times a day. Most everyone who was in Vietnam recognizes the Chicken Man call. *Bawk, Bawk, Bawk, Bawk*. Sometimes we'd be on a long flight somewhere with the FM radio off and with the other communication radios quiet. It could get a little boring. All of a sudden someone would broadcast in the clear on our communication radio, "Bawk, Bawk, Bawk, Bawk." We would all smile and get a chuckle. You've got to break the boredom and have some chuckles sometimes.

As time came closer to Christmas Day, our higher-ups, likely all the way to the President, decided that all the American armed forces in Vietnam needed a Christmas truce. A Christmas break. *They were so thoughtful!* This was supposedly also agreed to by enemy higher-ups. *Do you think they were actually talking? It was politics after all.*

We stopped all combat operations for about a week over Christmastime. The VC and NVA could have cared less about the holiday of course, but they sure loved the truce. They took full advantage of the break in American operations and the ceasefire to rearm and resupply all over Vietnam. Reports were that the Ho Chi Minh Trail was busy. We kept our side of the bargain by not flying any combat missions. There was no bombing, shooting of artillery or any ground action. Our military still flew reconnaissance flights to keep track of what was going on, however, and there was some spotty action on occasion if a base came under attack somewhere. But it was quiet for the most part. Of course, we took this time to work on our gunships to bring them back to full fighting condition. There were no Christmas trees or decorations, no singing and no special Christmas dinner. The slower pace during the down time was nice though.

After the truce ended we went back to the usual action trying to kill communists, or at least make life difficult for them. There were now more VC and NVA in our area and they were better armed and equipped. The time off from flying was nice. We also needed to give the bad guys a time out, to be good sports!

New Years' Eve was an interesting experience and one I'll never forget. We were especially vulnerable to attack by the VC during this holiday period since they knew we would be celebrating and our guard might be down. We still had our own guards on one side of our unit around the clock, on the northwest corner of the base. If we ever came under attack the established procedure was for the guards to fire red flares into the air signaling an attack, then open fire on the attackers with all the weapons they had available. Since everyone in our unit was so close to the perimeter, about fifty yards away, if we came under attack all of us would get our personal weapons that we kept in our hooches and join in defending our unit and the base.

On New Year's Eve 1969, everyone had planned to go to the EM Club or Officers' Club to eat, drink and bring in the New Year. I considered going with everyone else, but at the last minute decided to stay in my hooch, kick back and enjoy the quiet time with everyone gone. I'd write some letters home, read and hit the sack early. I was tired and not much of a party type anyway. Remember I was called Wild Bill.

While in my hooch alone writing a letter, a sergeant came to my door from out of nowhere, knocked, and asked if he could talk to me. I'd never met him before but I said, "Of course, come in." He was perhaps ten or fifteen years older than me. He said he just needed to talk to someone. Because I was an officer, I guess he figured he could talk to me. And I was the only one around. It quickly became obvious that he was homesick. We talked for a while. He cried some. There was some talk of his home and family, where we were and why, and some words of comfort were offered. After a short time he started feeling better. He soon said thanks and left. He was never seen again. It was like some phantom had materialized from thin air then departed. Being half a world away from everyone and everything one has ever known could be challenging and stressful at times, especially around holidays.

I wrote a letter home, read for a while then crawled into bed under my mosquito net around 11 o'clock. I fell sound asleep. All was quiet and dead still.

Suddenly, I was awakened out of a sound sleep to red flares streaking high across the dark sky and many automatic weapons on our perimeter firing, with red tracer bullets zipping through the air everywhere. Not knowing immediately what was going on I was always primed to react. We were under attack! Our base had been attacked the year before about this time, with many Americans killed and several helicopters blown up. Rolling out of bed with a sense of urgency, I pulled my steel pot (helmet) off the wall where it usually hung, grabbed my flack jacket and put it on, and got my pistol belt and pistol out of the bottom drawer of my dresser. The trusty rusty .38 caliber revolver was loaded and strapped around my waist. All this was done in bare feet and in my BVD's. A real warrior! I crawled on the floor to the door at the end of our hooch facing the perimeter where all the action was taking place. My loaded pistol was drawn and in my hand ready to extend my arm, aim and shoot.

At this point the realization struck that everyone was gone except me, that I was alone. I was only partially awake. My ability to resist attackers would not amount to much if Charlie began sneaking through our area. A view of them approaching in their conical reed hats and black pajamas between our tents, carrying their AK 47's, flashed across my mind. If our perimeter was overrun, all I could do was get as many of them as possible before they got me. I was crouched at the door ready to shoot if someone walked by. Again the realization struck that everyone was gone, there was no one here but me and the guards on the perimeter. No bad guys so far. Interesting.

The firing continued. Some bullets from machine gun fire actually hit our steel roof over my head and the red tracer bullets kept streaking through the air. Then the firing began to slow down. Still no bad guys. It seemed a bit strange somehow, but our guards must be doing their job and holding them off.

As my mind began to clear from the initial shock and I became more fully awake, it occurred to me that this was New Year's Eve. Looking at my watch, it was 12:05. Then it hit me. *Wow, you idiot!* All the firing and red flares were most certainly being fired in celebration of the New Year. Then looking at myself, I began to feel really silly: sleepy eyed, steel helmet, flac jacket, in my underwear, crouched down by the door, holding a loaded pistol. And yet, I still crawled out on the stoop outside, half expecting to see a bad guy sneaking by. By now I was almost hoping!

A few minutes later after all the firing had stopped, some of our guys began staggering back into our area, obviously heavily under the influence. A couple of guys walked by me and gave me a strange look. They probably thought they weren't seeing straight or that I was more under the influence than they were. They cautiously continued on by. The sight must have been very strange indeed. I finally walked back into my hooch, carefully unloaded my trusty Smith and Wesson, took care of everything, and crawled back in bed, but I didn't sleep the rest of the night. Nobody ever said anything to me the next day or later. Strange things sometimes happened in Vietnam. It was just another normal day in screwed up paradise.

CHAPTER 18

GOING HOME

By this time I was getting short, meaning it was just a few weeks until my scheduled return to the States. The normal routine was that pilots would stop flying on combat operations a week or so before scheduled departure. It was to avoid possible injury or death with just a few days remaining in country. It was not a good deal for a family to lose a son, father or husband anytime of course, but it was especially bad if it occurred right before they were expected home. Hope had gradually built up over the year for a safe return. Many guys were still wounded or killed a few weeks before their return home, of course. It happened all the time. Some guys were killed early on in combat operations shortly after they reported in country for duty. That didn't seem quite as bad somehow. If we had made it all the way through the year it was different.

We gunship pilots actually stopped flying on combat operations sooner than other pilots since the nature of our work was considered more dangerous. I stopped flying in early January, about three weeks before my date to return stateside.

With no more flying scheduled, I was assigned another extra duty in addition to Awards and Decorations Officer. The task was to write, publish and distribute a manual called *Aero Weapons*

Platoon Tactical Operations, something our unit and gun platoon did not have. Visiting and looking around at other units, another similar operations manual was found to use as a guide. The manual was worked on every day and was published and distributed the week before my leaving Vietnam. Although I can't remember everything that was in the manual, it covered such things as configuration and capabilities of different weapons systems, tactical situations where weapons systems were best applied, how to attack different targets, application of the combination of the various weapons, conservation of fire power, altitudes and flight patterns for different types of attacks, supporting troop lift flights, supporting other ground operations, hazards and precautions, emergency response procedures, along with many other things. It was interesting working on the manual but, at this point, I just wanted the time to pass and head back to the States.

Applying for some additional awards for some of our guys during this time and traveling to Battalion headquarters to follow up, I found that there still wasn't much interest in our pilots being recognized for some exceptional actions. All I saw at Battalion was higher rank, coffee cups, and what appeared to be complacency and politics. They appeared to be just a pathetic bunch of back scratchers! Those administrative coffee drinker types should go flying with us on some low level combat missions. It's obvious that all wars or conflicts become administrative and political in nature when individuals are advanced to jobs above actual combat action. That's perhaps the way it needs be.

I began organizing a few items to take home and prepared to catch a courier flight back to Saigon to the 90th Replacement Battalion, the same place I was processed through on the way in to Vietnam a year earlier. Orders were in hand for travel back to Travis Air Force Base in California with thirty days leave. Final packing was done, which wasn't much (my civilian shoes had long ago rotted away) and I said my good-byes to a few guys who had become closer friends. The next morning I went to the courier pad on base, jumped on a courier flight to Saigon, and strapped in the back as a passenger. As we lifted off and began climbing to altitude heading north, I turned and looked one last time at Can Tho, the home where everything had been put on the line, and where life had become very familiar and comfortable. I recalled some of the interesting and exciting times and the guys who had become like brothers. It was almost sad to be leaving. Almost. I still miss it today, actually.

The courier flight back to Saigon was more than just of casual concern to me. Once again, we were flying single ship without any gun escort, over territory that was not always friendly. An abundance of caution was part of my makeup after the last year. Something bad could still happen. The flight to Saigon wasn't quite as exciting as my first flight down to Dong Tam a year previous. We made it okay though. We landed on a helipad near downtown and I made my way to the Replacement Battalion. It was the initial first small step on the long road home.

I arrived at the processing center a little early. Many guys from my flight school that I had gone over with, finally began arriving. While sitting in a lounge area over an afternoon as more guys trickled in, we began to talk about where we ended up and our experiences. Later in the afternoon we noticed that some guys were missing. Different guys in the group spoke up when others asked what happened to the missing guys. Collectively we found out what happened to most of our missing buddies from flight school. Joe, the guy from Lansing that I went over with, didn't make it. It was the first I'd heard. He was hit by enemy fire flying a light observation helicopter, then crashed and burned. I still owed him twenty-five dollars from when we were last in San Francisco together. There were several other guys identified that were missing. It was a somber time. Later we sat through several debriefing meetings.

A day later we walked up the stairs onto a commercial air liner at Tan Son Nhat airport in Saigon and prepared to take off heading back to the U.S. and home. We all looked outside as we taxied toward the active runway for takeoff. *Goodbye, Vietnam!* We were soon rolling down the runway and finally blasted off on our freedom bird, climbing east toward home. After gaining a few thousand feet of altitude, thinking we might finally have made it out, we all looked around at each other. Smiles began to show and we let out a loud cheer. After all the near misses, being exposed to enemy gunfire every day and being shot up and shot down, we were finally safely departing Vietnam.

The flight back to Travis Air Force Base, northeast of San Francisco, California, was a very long flight. We stopped in Tokyo for refueling. Overall, it took about twenty hours. We finally stepped off the airplane on American soil at night, gone a lifetime it seemed, but just a year. Some guys went down on hands and knees at the bottom of the exit stairs and kissed the ground.

Travel from Travis Air Force Base to the San Francisco International Airport, then on home, was another adventure. The details are a bit fuzzy in my memory but there are still some things that are stuck my head like it was yesterday. I was traveling alone, and felt alone. Joe was not with me this time. I hired a taxi at Travis Air Force Base to take me to the San Francisco International airport. It was late at night. I was by myself in the back of the taxi. The taxi driver and I talked only briefly a couple of times.

Soaking up the first feelings of being back in the states and smelling the sweet air through open windows, I took in all the sights in that were available in the dark. As we came out of the hills on the north side of the Oakland Bay Bridge and headed down, San Francisco came into view across the bay all lit up. It was the first real view of the U.S. since leaving for Vietnam more than a year before. The sight has stuck with me to this day.

Sitting there in the quiet taxi in the dark, it suddenly struck me that I had made it back. *Or maybe I had.* It was unbelievable, almost too good to be true. *It was dark and quiet, maybe it was just a dream.* Moving around grabbing my arms and pinching myself, I needed to confirm that what was being experienced was real. *Back in one piece. That was something that I had not expected.* I had the feeling of being alone and vulnerable. The place where I'd been, the guys I'd lived with for a year and formed strong bonds with were suddenly missing. My previous home and intense exciting life had been stripped from me. It was a strange new land somehow. Maybe all the protests against the war that I heard and seen in the past and the loud negative voices toward the military was part of the feeling. I also did not have my loaded personal weapon with me and I felt naked.

I determined then and there, in that moment, to live my new life to the fullest and do what I chose to do, not controlled by or manipulated by other people. This was a vow to myself that would be violated a few times in later years when I was working for others in business. There was new unlimited freedom. The thought and profound feeling was that life is short and not at all certain from one moment to the next, even back home. A new lease on living had been offered. It was a new beginning. It almost felt like a rebirth. I could easily have been long since dead and gone for any number of reasons, something that would not have been any surprise to anyone in our line of work.

As we neared the airport's main terminal building, the taxi driver mentioned that the Hell's Angels were having some sort of rally at the airport and could be stirring up some trouble. There were extra police around. We pulled up in front of the entrance doors, I paid the taxi driver and got out. Grabbing my bag I walked into the terminal building dressed in my uniform. Alone and very military looking, I'm sure I stuck out like a sore thumb. I went to the ticket counter got a ticket to Kalamazoo and headed toward my departure gate.

Some Hell's Angels were around as well as many other passengers coming and going. No one seemed to pay any attention to me, which was a real relief. Neither did anyone make any eye contact. I was as concerned in that situation as at certain times in Vietnam in the heat of battle with bullets flying. A weapon was not available with which to respond if necessary. Strange. There were stories about Vietnam soldiers returning home that were yelled at, spat on and called baby killers. All went well for me, however, with no incidents. It was like I wasn't even seen. *Maybe I was a ghost and not actually alive after all. I was sort of just floating around it seemed.*

Finally departing from San Francisco, we headed nonstop to Detroit then would make a plane change to a much smaller twin turboprop commuter plane to Kalamazoo. The smell for the passengers around me might have been interesting, as I was perhaps a bit ripe by now, but it was of little concern to me. My clothes had been worn for a couple days and had last been hand washed next to my hooch, by Vietnamese women with water from the Mekong River.

It was winter and there was a blizzard blowing. My flight from Detroit made it as far as Jackson where the pilot had to land due to bad weather in Kalamazoo. From there I was loaded on a van with a few other passengers and driven to Kalamazoo. It had been a very long and tiring trip from my previous home at Can Tho, South Vietnam.

My wife and daughter, my folks and my younger brother and sister were at the airport at Kalamazoo to meet me. It was good to finally be back. That time is all foggy in my memory, having been sitting or standing for more than thirty hours by then, with little to eat or drink. Looking back I was beyond tired and perhaps not fully conscious. There is no recollection of the ride back to Cloverdale where my folks lived.

The next few days at my folks' place were somewhat puzzling. The feelings experienced during my travel home were a little unsettling. I was home but somehow felt very much out of place. I had suddenly been totally removed from the warm tropical environment and the intense activity that had become normal to me with guys who had become family. I was no doubt suffering some withdrawal symptoms. It was good to be home, but not all that good.

There weren't many questions asked or much curiosity expressed by my folks or wife concerning my activities or what was experienced during my year away. There hadn't been much information offered in letters sent home throughout the year. The seeming lack of interest was puzzling. There was a lot they didn't know and there was a lot more to tell. Maybe it was too soon. Questions at that time might have felt awkward to them. I could also have been acting a little strange. It felt to me as though I'd just come back from a week up north deer hunting and returned without a deer. *A lot of game had been bagged actually in the last year.* Maybe it was the weather. I'd been in a warm sunny tropical environment and now it was cold and dark. Michigan can be somewhat bleak in the winter. I had made it back and guess that's all that mattered at that point.

Arriving back home was uneventful as it turned out and sort of a disappointing experience. After past activities, the related risks and having looked forward to the return home, greater excitement had been anticipated. The whole time in Vietnam may have numbed or desensitized me more than I was aware.

I brought home only a couple of souvenirs other than some military patches and such. More could have been brought more home but I didn't go off base much and didn't specifically look for things to drag home. One souvenir I brought home was from Vung Tau, the city where I lived while in Cobra School. It was a beautiful hand stitched silk lounging jacket that had been embroidered with colorful birds and flowers. Everything was hand made by the Vietnamese even the woven buttons. I gave it to my wife after carrying it halfway around the world. She tried it on once, didn't like it, and I never saw her wear it after that. It's not like it was in style, especially considering the sentiment in the country at the time. She also may have thought I got it from a girlfriend. The general reputation of military guys overseas may have preceded me. I have no idea where it is today.

A hand painted silk picture was bought one day from a local guy when we were shut down between missions up in Tan An, a small village north of our base. Whenever we were on the ground shut down for some amount of time, locals would come around and try to sell us things. This day I bought a colorful Bengal tiger hand painted on silk. It was beautiful. It is still beautiful today and it is framed and hanging in our home. It's a very special and valuable item, at least to me.

CHAPTER 19

EVERY WAKE-UP IS A GOOD DAY

Having returned home and adjusting to my new environment over several days, it was time to look ahead to my next duty station, Ft. Rucker, Alabama. Orders were received and my young family and I packed up and headed south. Back to where it was warm.

My daughter was a very different little girl to me when I returned. When I left for Vietnam she was eight months old and just crawling and now she was almost two years old and was walking. Her mother dressed her in cute little dresses. She was really cute. She had no idea who I was after my long absence and initially didn't want anything to do with me, which was no surprise. One entire year had passed with me being gone during a very formative period in her young life. But she warmed up to me gradually and we got reacquainted.

The balance of my active duty commitment was at Ft. Rucker for the next ten months or so. Since having only a few months left on active duty before scheduled departure, I would not be given the desired flight instructor duty at Ft. Rucker, but rather was assigned as a platform instructor with the Academic Instructor Training Branch, AITB. I taught a number of public speaking and lecturing type classes in our two week course to students who would become platform instructors around base in various units. I also went with other members of my training branch to different units around base weekly, sat in on classes and evaluated instruction given by previous students that had gone through our course.

After Vietnam, the duty at Ft. Rucker was not very challenging. We took long lunches, played games in our training building during the day between periods of work, took Wednesday's off to play golf, and took Friday afternoon's off for happy hour at the officers' club. It was a relaxing respite after my previous duty overseas but it quickly became boring.

During this second tour at Ft. Rucker, I seriously considered staying in the military and making it a career. All the necessary paperwork was completed to sign up for a life-long career in the Army. With my Aviation Engineering Degree, graduating at the top in flight school, having volunteered for Vietnam, and with very high officer efficiency evaluations, my acceptance into the Army full time was a certainty. I was told that eventual assignment to the helicopter development command was a real possibility. All the paperwork was endorsed up through channels and ended up at the Pentagon. Having a direct WATTS telephone line to the Pentagon, I was able to talk to my branch placement people anytime to discuss my future prospects in the Army. I talked to them several times. After current duty at Ft. Rucker, I would be sent to career officer advanced school for nine months then likely go back to Vietnam for another year as an airmobile commander. At this time civilian work was also being considered. Having a wife and young daughter, the prospect of soon returning to Vietnam was not appealing, plus my wife did not like military life with the frequent moves.

I was offered a job with Aladdin Industries in Nashville and decided to take it, so we were to leave military active duty. Less than a year later I would be calling the Pentagon trying to get back in the military. But the decision had been made at that point and a return to active duty was not possible.

After leaving the active duty military in December 1970, we moved to Nashville, Tennessee, where I had accepted a job offer with Aladdin Industries as a production supervisor. I continued to fly helicopters as a gun platoon commander with the Tennessee National Guard.

The most important event of our few years in Tennessee was the birth of our son. He was born in Nashville in early 1972, during the time when U.S. involvement in Vietnam was beginning to wind down. Our new son was a perfect little tike. I was glad to have been around to help him come into this world. It was meant to be, I was not just a ghost after all.

The entire experience during my year in Vietnam was fascinating in many ways. It was a beautiful country, the people were beautiful, the culture and history were rich, and the interaction with the Vietnamese people was interesting. The flying was great experience, the combat action was challenging and at times quite scary, but often rather fun. This sort of flying experience couldn't possibly be bought back stateside. It's only available in a combat zone.

My experience in Vietnam left me with some immediate feelings and impressions upon returning home, as well as longer lasting feelings and impressions. Vietnam was an exciting place: the travel to and from, the sights and sounds, the people, the camaraderie, the combat action, the near misses, the challenge involved in flying, the inflight emergencies, and much more. All of it was exciting. Due to the nature of the work, for which I was well trained and was mentally prepared, I did not expect with any certainty to survive my tour in Vietnam. Many like me didn't. I had decided early on to just accept whatever happened. What real choice did one actually have anyway?

It was a very uneventful return back to the States for me, after living through a series of truly life changing experiences over a significant period of time. Home was quiet, dull and boring. There seemed to be little interest by anyone about my experiences over the past year. I've met and talked with other Vietnam helicopter pilots and other veterans over the years. We always felt an almost immediate and special bond with each other, often identifying similar feelings that we had upon returning home. These men were usually total strangers, and yet we would talk and we knew we were understood. One had to be there. It's been like this to the present day. No one who wasn't there can understand, and I've learned that there's no point making much effort trying to explain. Like with many Vietnam veterans, the topic often is just left alone, and we don't talk much about our time back then.

One of my immediate impressions after returning home was how absolutely spoiled rotten Americans were. They very much took for granted the peaceful, safe and secure environment they lived in, and all the luxuries they had. It really struck me how upset and angry some people could become over truly meaningless trivial little things. I would often just smile cynically and shake my head. Some Americans could be really pathetic. Many adults would act like immature spoiled brats. And we wonder why some kids grow up today having problems with all their toys and excess luxuries. We can often still see the same silly, stupid, childish attitudes in Americans today. There's nothing like living in some poor, third world country, or serving in a combat zone to get a good dose of reality and appreciate simple things in life. Everyone should experience some hardship or live close enough to it to learn to be thankful for what they have. Americans tend to think too much of themselves with their own self-centered perception. There are exceptions, of course, with many individuals having a larger more informed view of the world and our place in it.

My experience in Vietnam caused me to develop real empathy for the Vietnamese people, often living close to them and working among them. They are a beautiful, ancient people in a beautiful land. They have been innocent victims of cruel periods of conflict for decades under the United States, the French and further back. The United States no doubt did a better job of being cruel than the French. Our footprint was much larger. The peaceful Vietnamese people had to be on our side, smiling at us and working with us during the day, and then on the side of the communist forces at night just to have some hope of surviving. And many innocent people did not survive.

It also struck me how Americans could be so shallow, self-centered and egotistical. The Vietnamese people always impressed me as being very polite and humble. The United States military forces offered nothing better to the Vietnamese people that I could see. We polluted their country, destroyed their landscape, fouled their culture, and hurt them in many ways. Our presence there caused pretty Vietnamese girls to try to make up their eyes so they would look round like Americans and wear miniskirts like American girls. Many were pretty but it was sad to see. I very much preferred their slanted eyes and beautiful traditional dress.

While hurting the Vietnamese people, we were of course engaged in an effort that had broader global significance. Our politicians, at least for a while, obviously considered our efforts worthwhile. Chinese and Russian regimes were involved. Remember the times, communist leaders were pounding their shoes on the table and threatening world domination. The only lasting justification for the United States having been in Vietnam may be that we simply delayed the spread of communism in Southeast Asia for a time.

Another impression that struck me, after a lot of experience in combat operations, was just how cheap life could be. Life in general, Vietnamese lives and our own, somehow did not have quite as much value in a place like Vietnam at the time. Life as we were living it could end in the blink of an eye. We all accepted the real possibility of losing our most prized possession. It wasn't that one's own life and the lives of those around us weren't considered important and weren't valued. Much to the contrary. We all worked hard to survive and live. We valued our own lives and did everything we could to stay alive.

At times we experienced firsthand how cheap life could be. It was a growing impression as my year progressed. American lives as well as Vietnamese lives, friend or foe, sometimes seemed almost temporary somehow. Some amount of death was anticipated and expected. It was real combat after all. Frank, Joe, Bill and many others were gone quickly, and while we were saddened by the loss we were not particularly surprised or shocked. Many young Vietnamese people were killed one day south of our base and were thrown into the back of a dump truck. Who knew for sure if they were good guys or bad guys? Each individual was worth one black mark on my windshield.

A helicopter pilot from our base was flying south of our base one day and his helicopter blew up in midair. The VC, probably on our base during the day, had at some point dropped a hand grenade in his fuel tank. He was gone in a split second. One afternoon after missions were completed, one of our crewmen was on top of his running helicopter pouring a bucket of water into the inlet of his jet engine to clean it, and without thinking stood up. A rotor blade hit him in the head killing him instantly and he tumbled to the ground. Other people died almost daily. Many of our guys were injured or wounded and disappeared from our unit. After a while living in this environment one began to not take life too seriously.

I've often said, "Life is a relative thing." Most people don't understand what is said in that statement, a little play on words perhaps. If we really think about it, we consider life truly important and valuable only as it relates to immediate relatives and others close around us who we know. Just a few people. Beyond these few, it appears there is not great importance placed on life. Dying is commonplace and is indeed part of life itself. Nature's way. We may sincerely say we value all life, but absent the close connection to someone personally life doesn't mean quite so much to us. Hundreds of people die in automobile accidents every day in this country and we hardly take notice. There are countless numbers of others dying around us all the time for various reasons and we pay little attention. In general most people feel that life is valuable and precious however. It certainly is to me. Some of us have experienced another side a little more close up however. Life, as precious as it is, can seem cheap sometimes.

I was happy of course to have survived my time in Vietnam. My life and the lives of those around me are important and have great value. I am able to see the larger picture though, and keep everything sort of in perspective.

Yet another strong impression of mine that developed in Vietnam, and one that has remained to this day, was just how inhumane man can be to his fellow man. It made, and still makes, no sense to me how our supposedly rational-thinking human race can be so shortsighted and absolutely stupid. It's nothing new, of course, but humans should be smarter. Idealism is an easy thought process. Politicians and those in power should aspire to higher ideals. Politicians, individuals, and those in organized religions can brutalize each other often seemingly taking pleasure in seeing others suffer. Sometimes our missions drew us into activities that resulted in man being inhumane to his fellow man, but I took no pleasure in it. Peace and love are the more noble pursuits for the human race, it seems to me. We're all in this together, and we should join hands instead of lifting a fist and striking each other. Make love not war. It's become a timeless expression. If some would only listen. Maybe I should become an old hippy. Part way there!

Survivor guilt has sometimes been an issue for combat veterans returning home from combat experience. This has not been a problem for me personally. A veteran was once asked if he suffered from survivor guilt and his response was, "No, because I was there." This is an interesting perspective. I put everything on the line in Vietnam every day that I flew and survived. It was not my time to go.

Some of our less than honorable politicians, past and present, should be feeling a lot of guilt for their greedy self-serving ways while sending young Americans overseas to die in political conflicts. Some recent politicians used money and influence to avoid serving in Vietnam. Despicable! We should be proud of and support other more honorable politicians who answered the call and served their country in Vietnam and other wars.

There has been some bad feeling and perhaps a little guilt regarding the Vietnamese people. Surviving my involvement in combat operations throughout the year then returning home in one piece, an injustice was felt. I was alive when hundreds of Vietnamese were dead by my hand. Being good at what we did and with body count a desired number on the scoreboard, it somehow didn't seem quite fair. True, they may have been considered the enemy, but they were all just human beings caught up in the conflict trying to survive like the rest of us. They had wives and family back home too. The feeling was that perhaps I should have paid my dues and done my part. The nature of any military conflict however involves doing your job and surviving if you can.

As a result of my experience in Vietnam, I've always had a soft spot for Vietnamese people. Looking back at them it's easy to see beautiful, ancient, and humble people, people that should not have been made to suffer for some greater perceived good from outsiders. Not all Vietnam veterans feel the same for sure.

Immediately after returning home boredom began growing and became an issue to deal with. Considerable boredom became common place and was understandable. I missed the intense activity, the risk and the shock of combat action. Some of the feeling was likely due to not having my regular dose of adrenaline. Adrenaline is an exciting, driving natural drug. There's no way to get it though unless you're doing something exciting, living on the edge.

Work at my next, and final, duty station, Ft. Rucker, was as a classroom instructor. The job was challenging in some ways which was good, but overall I was bored stiff. It became obvious to me why some guys who had completed their tour in Vietnam in my unit had returned before I left. To be able to have gone back to Vietnam would have been great. With a wife and young daughter, however, it was time to place priority on their welfare and to stay home.

A general sense of boredom has stuck with me through the years and still has to be dealt with off and on. I took additional civilian flight training in Ozark, Alabama a small town just east of Ft. Rucker. Commercial and multiengine airplane ratings were gained there. A Mooney Executive 21 was rented once and we flew back home to Michigan on leave for a couple of weeks. Other types of airplanes have been owned over the years and involved some flying that was considered by some to be a little risky. To me it was just challenging and a little more sporting. All flying is risky actually. But I am a good pilot, am conservative and know my own limitations.

At one time my wife told me that what I needed was for her to chase me around the yard shooting at me with a shotgun. Her observation was interesting at the time, many years after my tour of duty in Vietnam. It would have been exciting but it likely would not have come to a good end. She might have been especially motivated and she might have been a good shot!

Another issue we hear a lot about today is PTSD, Post Traumatic Stress Disorder. A condition first identified and recognized among veterans from the Vietnam conflict. I've never been particularly bothered by my Vietnam experience, although it's pretty well accepted that all combat veterans are affected in some ways. Sleeping has never been a problem and there have never been troublesome nightmares. There have been dreams about Vietnam though. After returning home, and for some years thereafter, I would react to sudden loud noises. A slamming door would immediately set me on edge, on guard ready to act. I have also acted out in other ways in the past, due perhaps in part to the overall stress experienced in Vietnam. It was fortunate for me to have been able to fly in Vietnam. Combat operations could be left behind at the end of a day, flying back to our base and some semblance of a normal life. I also didn't have to get my hands too dirty cleaning up the messes we made.

Something no one has known, except my wife, Margaret, is that a few years ago I visited our local recruiting office and inquired about going back into the military to help in Iraq. Officially still in the military, I still have the permanent rank of Captain. Flying at my age would not have been an option but there might have been some opportunity to work in some aviation related area. It might have been just a short vacation of sorts while providing some worthwhile service. As suspected, my age ruled out my going back in. We're only as old as we think, they say. We're usually much older than we think though.

A fair amount of reading about Vietnam and other wars has been commonplace for me in recent years. Everything read offers some additional insight into the periods before, during and after for many veterans of combat action. Reading offers words and prompts thoughts that are sometimes difficult to come up with to describe one's feelings.

One recent reading pretty accurately explains some of the feelings people like me had upon returning home from Vietnam, and explains in part why many guys previously from my unit in Vietnam returned to action after only a few months away. Over there one was exposed to the day to day risks typical in a combat environment and the very real prospect of injury or death. We were part of a closely knit expertly functioning unit, routinely involved in life and death activities. We felt like somebody. We felt important and had especially strong bonds with the people we worked with around us. We were living on the edge and were an important part of a grand operational endeavor. We were alive.

Then we went home. When we got home we found life was as we left it in most respects. Everyone expected us to fit right back in as if nothing had happened. But something big *had* happened. Most around us didn't know that or couldn't see it. And something big was missing. All of a sudden all the friends we had developed close bonds with and had survived with were gone. There was no more life on the edge with life or death experiences every day, and no more exciting flying. We were alone in a seemingly indifferent and very dull place, no longer quite fitting in.

In Vietnam we were "somebody", and back home we were "nobody". The feeling of being a "nobody" after returning home may have been reinforced at the time by the sentiment in the country regarding the Vietnam experience and those who participated in it. I never had anyone call me a baby killer, although unknowingly I probably was, or spit at me, but I have come across some people who clearly did not want to associate with me when they discovered I was a Vietnam veteran. Some people with their small minds and complete lack of understanding apparently just can't get beyond it. There have also been a few people like the riding stable operator on a trail up in the remote mountains in Belize, who upon hearing that I had served in Vietnam, immediately said *thank you* without needing to hear more. It was a very unexpected and meaningful comment coming from him at the time. Other statements of thanks in more recent times just seem to be patronizing somehow and are not necessary. I don't need to hear it.

Upon returning from Vietnam I became increasingly more independent, strong minded, cynical and short tempered. The strong inner strength developed was likely the result of having worked routinely in potentially deadly endeavors. A very personal thing. There's not much that gets to me or bothers me very much today, other than a bad golf game. I tend to be quiet and somewhat distant. Individual responsibility is a big issue with me and I'm not tolerant of pettiness. I don't suffer idiots well, and there seem to be plenty around. I can come across as ruthless at times.

Thorough training in the military began with early basic training and continued beyond. The basic mission of any military combat force is to seek out and destroy the enemy. All military training supports this basic mission with a broad variety of strategies. I was taught how to use a bayonet on the end of a rifle, how to kill with a knife, and how to use a variety of other weapons. The basics. Hand to hand combat training included how to take down and disable an opponent. The concept of fair play was never a part of any training. Whatever the weapon used, the objective was to kill your enemy before he kills you. It can often come down to this basic struggle. In flight school we not only had training in flying helicopter gunships but also training in survival, escape and evasion specific to our future flying in Vietnam. We learned the operation and application of all the weapons systems available on gunships. A lot of experience was had in Vietnam with use of the tools of my trade. This sort of activity can, over a period of time, harden one to a significant degree. I am basically a sensitive and caring person but don't always show it outwardly naturally, or very well.

I once met with an Air National Guard commander at an Air Force base on a small business matter. We got to talking about flying in Vietnam. He had flown over there also. We talked for a few minutes about where we had flown and some of our experiences. After a few minutes he hesitated, looked me straight in the eyes and said, "You're lucky to be alive." I replied, "Yes sir, I am." He understood.

It's now been over forty years since my time in Vietnam and life is good. For me now the whole Vietnam experience is a collection of memories from the distant past that are becoming dimmer as time marches on. Not that I don't remember, but the memories are some greater distance away and the action not quite so much like it happened yesterday.

Every wake-up is a good day.

GLOSSARY

ARVN -	An abbreviation for the Army Republic of Vietnam. Our allies.
AO -	Area of Operation. Any combat operational area.
Bunker -	Any protective shelter either U.S., Vietnamese, or enemy, designed to protect people from weapons fire from rifle, machine gun, mortars, rockets, bombs, etc.
Boonies -	Any area out in the countryside not part of a town or city.
C&C -	Command and Control. Flown in a helicopter at altitude where air mobile operations were commanded. *Not Canadian Club and Coke!*
Charlie -	A name given by U.S. forces to North Vietnam troops and the Viet Cong.
Class 6 -	The Army department on base that sold all drinks, Coke, beer, etc.
Click -	One kilometer of distance on the ground. Like our mile, but metric and shorter (about 0.6 mile).
DG -	Directional Gyro. A compass type navigational instrument in aircraft.
Duce & ½ -	A big, heavy, rugged, two and one-half ton flatbed truck.
EGT -	Exhaust Gas Temperature, measured out the back of a jet engine.

EOD - Explosive Ordinance Demolition. The team that recovered explosives or destroyed items by blowing them up.

Flechette - A small brass dart contained in the warhead of some rockets.

Free Fire Zone - Any suspected enemy area that was open to firing of weapons anytime with out consideration for rules of engagement.

GCA - Ground Controlled Approach. A radar approach system used in bad weather.

Gunship - A helicopter equipped with various weapons system that was used for air to ground weapons fire instead of carrying troops.

Hooch - Any dwelling, building, or room, where Americans or Vietnamese lived.

Huey - As in the Huey helicopter built by Bell Helicopters. The "C" model was only one specific model used as a gunship

LOH - Light Observation Helicopter. Its role was scouting and/or command work and didn't carry significant weapons or troops.

LST - A Navy ship used to haul munitions to our bases.

LZ - Landing Zone, anyplace combat troops were landed for combat operations.

Mama San - A Vietnamese mother.

MPC - Military pay certificates that were all paper. Use as standard currency

Nomex - Fire retardant wool-like material used for flight suits.

NVA - North Vietnamese Army. The official army of communist North Vietnam that operated in South Vietnam along with the Viet Cong.

Papa San -	A Vietnamese father.
PIC -	Pilot in Command. Pilots that were in charge of the flight of their gunship.
PSP -	Perforated Steel Plate. It was linked together and was laid on the ground for airport runway surface.
PZ -	Pick up Zone. Any area where combat troops were picked up after combat operations.
Sampan -	The common wooden boat used for hauling people, wood, supplies, etc. It was powered either by outboard motor or by paddling.
Tunnel -	Underground passageways and rooms that helped the NVA and VC, as well as many Vietnamese civilians, hide from the Americans, move from place to place, store munitions, cook, sleep, and provide medical treatment.
VC -	Viet Cong, The local militia that worked mainly in South Vietnam with the North Vietnamese Army against the Americans.
VT fuse -	A Variable Time fuse that screwed on the nose of a rocket warhead.

Phil Hitchcock was born in Kalamazoo, Michigan in 1943. He Graduated from Western Michigan University with an aviation engineering degree in 1967.

Phil first became interested in flying during high school. He pursued his interest through college earning early pilot ratings, then joined the U.S. Army where he saw action as a combat helicopter gunship pilot in Vietnam in 1969.

Phil is now retired and enjoys the quiet country life in southern Michigan with his wife Margaret and their dog Animosh.

Contact Phil at: loonworksllc@gmail.com